WALKABOUT MALIBU TO MEXICO

Hiking Inn to Inn
on the Southern California Coast

Tom Courtney

Happy Hiking

Tom C try

WALKABOUT CALIFORNIA PRESS

Walkabout Malibu to Mexico: Hiking Inn to Inn on the Southern California Coast

1st EDITION 2014

Copyright © 2014 by Tom Courtney

Front Cover photos copyright © 2014 by Tom Courtney
Interior photos by author with Emily Courtney
Maps: Tom Courtney
Cover design: Crawshaw Design
Interior design and layout: Crawshaw Design, adapted from author's design

ISBN 978-0-9903926-0-6

Published by: **Walkabout California Press**
                  www.WalkaboutCalifornia.com

Cover photos: Front cover clockwise from upper left: Paradise Cove on the Exploring the Malibu Coast Walkabout, Crystal Cove Cabin on the Newport Beach to San Clemente Walkabout, Point Vicente on the Santa Monica to Santa Catalina Walkabout, El Matador State Beach on the Exploring the Malibu Coast Walkabout. *Back cover from left:* Avalon Bay Santa Catalina on the Santa Catalina to Newport Beach Walkabout, Terranea Terrace on the Santa Monica to Santa Catalina Walkabout, Point La Jolla on the Oceanside to La Jolla Walkabout.

Information contained in this book is correct to the best of the author's knowledge at date of publication. Author and publisher assume no liability for damages arising from errors or omissions.

Safety notice: Hiking the Pacific Coast can be a risky endeavor. Walkabout California Press and the author have strived to ensure that the information in this book is accurate at press time, but you must take responsibility for your health and safety while on these trail. Be prudent. Heed the cautions in this book, and check local conditions.

It takes a village. I am grateful to:

The Walkabout California Community. Thousands have hit the California trails to hike from inn-to-inn. They are an inspiration.

Emily Courtney, daughter, Walkabout California business manager, editor, strategist, negotiator, motivator. Her devotion, joy, persistence, and support made this project possible.

Lynn MacMichael, Howard Wiemer, and David Chatfield, my editorial team. What good friends and wise advisors.

Scott Jordan. We have rambled the coast and mountains of California. He joined me on two of these walkabouts. A good friend with an uncanny ability to find the best fish tacos.

Heidi Thompson, wife and ideal hiking companion. Always eager for adventure, she joined me for four of these walkabouts. She keeps my writing grounded and true.

"Walkabout Northern California: Hiking Inn to Inn has taken the European practice of trekking to food and rest without having to lug your load, and tailored it to our backyard...We're eager to check out the 2-day, 14-mile Mendocino Coast trip, with pygmy forests, stunning sea cliffs, and sun bathing sea otters. But more important: cozy beds, ocean views, and a spa day at the Little River Inn."
– Sunset Magazine

"Courtney's engaging descriptions include natural and human history and stories of quirky locals. He also provides route information, lodging recommendations, trailhead directions, sources for trail maps, and tips on gear and safety... the book offers rich experience: car-free rambles rewarded with creature comforts--perfect for aging backpackers, carbon-conscious travelers, and anyone interested in slowing down to appreciate nature and hospitality."
– Bay Nature

"...now comes a guide that brings readers both Courtney's savvy knowledge and firsthand experience of exploring 400 miles of California wilderness. Different from other hiking guides, this one provides readers with everything they need to turn their adventure into a true walkabout... It's a practical guide but also rich in detail. Courtney allows readers to see deep inside the wilderness of each hiking segment. He brings it to life, tempting all those who love the outdoors to see it for themselves."
– Contra Costa Times

"Nothing wrong with roughing it, of course but occasionally a guy likes to soak his weary feet in a hot tub, sip a fine merlot alongside a juicy steak, and sleep in high-thread-count sheets along the way."
– Sacramento Bee

"You wake up in your comfy room, eat a delicious breakfast, set off for the day through the beautiful wilds, and make it to the next lodging in time for cocktails. This type of traveling is fairly common in Europe, but not as popular here in the States... It might seem daunting to plan an inn-to-inn trip yourself, but Courtney offers detailed itineraries, complete with trail notes, suggested stops, lodging recommendations, and the like."
– Apartment Therapy

"Hikers who want to explore in greater depth such incredibly beautiful places as the Marin Coast, Monterey Bay, and Lassen National Park, will enjoy Courtney's book. It's a handy guide to the routes you'll be taking and he enriches your journey as he describes the natural and cultural history of the land."
– San Francisco Examiner

"Does your ideal multi-day hike end with a good meal, a glass of wine, and a comfortable bed? Check out Walkabout California, an itinerary planning site for hikers who want to travel light and stay at inns along the way."
– Weekend Sherpa

"You've done the head down, makeup smeared, high heels in the hand thing. Erase the memory with a different walk: some fresh air and some of NorCal's most breathtaking foot trails (and assurance that a cozy inn awaits you when your dogs start barkin') with Walkabout California... Hiking from inn to inn is great exercise (hello, supercalves) and is much more Earth-friendly than driving or even public transportation."
– Ideal Bite

Table of Contents

Introduction

"Wealth I ask not, hope nor love,
Nor a friend to know me;
All I ask, the heaven above
And the road below me."

- Robert Louis Stevenson, The Vagabond

Miles of
Uninterrupted Beach

"Above all, do not lose your desire to walk. Every day I walk myself into a state of well-being and walk away from every illness. I have walked myself into my best thoughts, and I know of no thought so burdensome that one cannot walk away from it."

- *Soren Kierkegaard, Letter to his neice, Henriette Lund, 1847*

TAKE A WALKING VACATION, hiking inn-to-inn on the Southern California Coast – a land of sublime swimming beaches, rugged rocky shores with surprisingly abundant wildlife, inviting seaside villages, great dining, and delightful inns. This walkabout stretches 200 miles from Leo Carrillo State Beach, near the L.A. and Ventura County line, to the border with Mexico. There are seven chapters, multi-day hikes stopping each night at a coastal inn for a comfortable bed, a hot shower, a good meal, and a glass of wine.

It was mid-June when my wife, Heidi, and I set out in a light morning haze to hike three days along the coast of Malibu. The fog burned off, and temperatures rose into the 70s. Beautiful beaches beckoned us to stop and swim – Trancas, Zuma, Paradise Cove, Escondido, Amarillo, Surfrider, Carbon, Topanga, Will Rogers, and Santa Monica. But, it was also a challenging hike. Rocky, isolated shorelines demanded bouldering. At times, our only companions were harbor seals and sea lions lounging on offshore outcroppings. Pelicans, cormorants, and shorebirds fed in the bountiful waters. A pod of dolphins glided by, just beyond the surf line, black dorsal fins cresting with each breath. We tried to hike around rugged promontories jutting out into the Pacific, but there were times when we needed to take brief strolls through residential neighborhoods before returning to the shore. In the evenings, we explored the restaurants and nightlife of Zuma Beach, Malibu, and Santa Monica.

Hermosa Beach Volleyball

This was really fun! Over the next two years, I returned to the coast with Heidi and friends to hike all the way to Mexico. To the east lay urban L.A and San Diego, but they are mostly out of sight and mind, cut off by high coastal bluffs. The dominant force is always the wild, powerful, untamed Pacific.

In this book, you will find everything you need to plan your own inn-to-inn hike: a detailed route; transportation information for reaching the trailhead and for getting back when you have finished the hike; sketch maps and suggestions for more detailed maps; lodging options with location, contact information, and prices. There is also a description of what to expect along the trail, reviews of inns and restaurants, and some history both natural and human.

Our route follows the coast, straying inland only when the

shoreline is blocked. Every section brings beauty, adventure, and surprises. Hike the coastal bluffs and rocky shores of the great isolated peninsulas – Palos Verdes and La Jolla. Stroll seductive beaches – Manhattan, Redondo, Huntington, San Clemente, Carlsbad. Explore wildlife preserves teeming with shorebirds along the

Crystal Cove State Beach

Pacific Flyway. Bypass uber industrial L.A. and Long Beach harbors by taking the ferry to Santa Catalina to hike her mountains, explore her coast by kayak, and to snorkel in Lover's Cove. Stay one night at a luxurious resort and the next in a friendly hostel. Enjoy the art scene of Laguna; the crazy people-watching of Venice Beach; the nightlife of Santa Monica, Newport Beach, and Coronado.

Explore and savor the magnificent Southern California Coast at two miles an hour. Take a walkabout – hiking inn-to-inn.

Best Seasons for Hiking the Coast
Have you ever tuned into Pasadena's Rose Parade on January 1 and

noticed it's almost always warm and sunny? The Southern California Coast is blessed with a Mediterranean climate – rain in the winter and sunny spring, summer, and fall.

Rainfall averages only 11-13 inches a year, but it can be monsoonal. Still, I don't discourage a winter inn-to-inn hike along the shore. The sky may open with a fierce storm that can soak you, but duck into a café to sit it out or put on your raingear and keep hiking. It will probably be over quickly, and the sun will soon come out. Winter mid-day temperatures average in the 60s.

Morning fog comes with the summer, and coastal residents speak of "June Gloom." Start your hike in the cool fog. It should burn off by late morning. Inland temperatures may reach 100, but expect highs in the 70s along the coast.

Winter and spring are great for having long stretches of shoreline all to yourself. Summer brings rising ocean temperatures. Average water temperatures climb from the low 60s in early summer to the high 60s and low 70s in August and September. Late summer and fall are wonderful for hiking and swimming.

We hiked from inn-to-inn along the coast during all four seasons. They each have a unique character and special gifts.

Maps

There is a simplified trail map for each day's hike. The Route at the end of each chapter will guide you around sections where you may need to leave the coast to walk bluff trails, residential streets, or on sidewalks or bike lanes along Pacific Coast Highway. It is also useful to consult other more detailed maps when planning your hike. The U.S. Geological Survey sells topographical hiking maps and provides free maps you can download. Visit ***http://store.usgs.gov*** and go to the map locator. The Maps section at the end of each chapter identifies the quadrants that apply to each day's hike.

Google Maps at *www.maps.google.com* is also a useful tool for viewing the shoreline and roadways adjacent to the shore. You may want to carry a good road map of the coast to pull out if the way through a residential neighborhood is confusing.

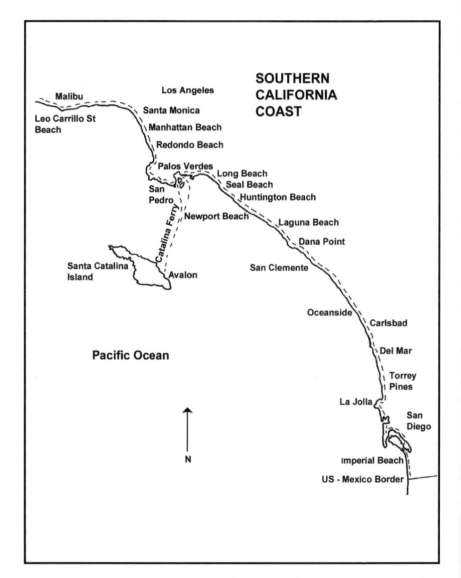

Moonrise over Hotel del Coronado

Safety

"Be not thou foolish; why shouldest thou die before thy time?"

– Ecclesiastes

The best safety precautions are to stay warm, dry, hydrated, rested, regularly fueled with food, and alert to the powerful Pacific. Taking these precautions will put you in the best position to manage any surprises.

Other safety measures:

Know the tide schedules. Read the trail description and The Route for each chapter to identify stretches that are difficult or impossible to hike if the tide is in. Time your hike to reach those spots at low tide. If your passage is blocked by high tides, take one of the frequent paths or public stairs to briefly walk residential streets or the sidewalk or bike lane along the highway, and then return to the beach. Tide schedules are available at ***http://tidesandcurrents.noaa. gov/tide_predictions.shtml.*** If you are hiking with a smart phone, download one of many free tide schedule apps.

Rock Shelves South Ocean Beach

Don't turn your back on the ocean. Rogue waves will soak your feet or worse. Every year unsuspecting beachgoers get knocked down and dragged out to sea by surprise surges.

Know your route. Study the sketch maps, The Route, and read the trail description before you leave. Carry an additional map or electronic device that can connect you to a map of the coastline and adjacent streets in case your passage is blocked by the tide.

Leave your itinerary with a friend or loved one. Let your innkeepers know that you are coming on foot, and give them a number to call if you don't arrive by a specified time. Check in with your friend or loved one along the way and call them when you finish, letting them know you are home safe.

Weather. Hiking the Southern California Coast is delightful any time of year. Prepare for cool foggy mornings in the summer with extra layers. Rain is possible October through March, and it can be torrential. There are occasional storms even when it is not rainy season. Check weather reports for rain, and bring your rain gear if it is predicted.

Take a cell phone. There is coverage with major carriers for most of the entire 200 mile route.

Take care with stream crossings. There are bridges over most rivers and estuary outlets. Some seasonal streams only reach the Pacific during rainy season. Look for a sandbar that forms where the stream meets the sea. You may be able to wade across. If a waterway looks dangerous, take the long route around. Hiking poles are helpful for maintaining balance on stream crossings.

Hike with a partner. You will hike remote and isolated rock shelves, boulder strewn shorelines, and long lonely beaches on many of these walkabouts. I am guilty of not always following this rule, but it is easier to get out of jam if you have someone to help you.

> *"Two are better than one; for if they fall, the one will lift up his fellow..."*
>
> *– Ecclesiastes*

What to Bring

Travel as light as possible.

Footwear: Light boots or hiking shoes work well on this terrain which varies from sandy beach, to rocky shoreline, to residential lane. Some distance hikers prefer hiking sandals, great for wading around a rocky point or for strolling through the shallows, but you need to enjoy the feel of hiking with sand in your shoes. I try to hike barefoot for a part of each day, slowing down to savor sea and sand.

Daypack: Choose a daypack that fits your shoulders and has a hip belt and sternum strap. Even with a light load, your shoulders will be grateful at the end of the day that you carried most of the weight on your hips. Once you are packed and ready, the pack should weigh 12-15 pounds. Try to resist the urge to fill it.

Terranea Terrace

Other essentials:

- One or two sets of hiking clothes, depending upon the length of the walkabout
- Extra socks and underwear that can easily be washed and dried overnight
- Hat with a brim
- Overshirt for warmth that is nice enough for dinner in a restaurant
- Sunglasses, sunscreen, and a small first-aid kit with adhesive pads for blisters
- Cell phone and charger
- Water
- Tide tables. You can find accurate tables at *http://tidesonline. nos.noaa.gov/geographic.html*
- Flashlight or headlamp
- Swimsuit for the beach, pool, or spa and a small towel
- Minimal toiletries because your inn should provide soap, shampoo, and lotion
- Lunch plus some high-energy trail bars or other trail snacks
- Multi-tool pocketknife

Optional items:

- An extra lightweight layer for warmth in the evening or through the fog
- A lightweight change of clothes for dinner
- Light sarong for beach lounging and toweling off
- Rain jacket during rainy season, small enough to fit into a small stuff sack
- Rain pants
- Insect repellent
- Bandana

Pacific Beach

- A few Ziploc plastic bags
- Binoculars
- Compass and maps
- Camera
- Extra batteries
- Paperback book or electronic reader
- A journal
- GPS receiver
- Waterproof matches or lighter
- Hiking poles

How to use this book

Each chapter's descriptive guide gives a sense of what to expect along the trail - the terrain, key landmarks, how to get around sections that are difficult or impossible to pass at high tide, suggestions on when to set out in order to time your hike to reach challenging sections at low tide, great swimming beaches, places to stop for lunch or to buy supplies, delightful spots for wild life viewing or people watching, reviews of inns and restaurants. It also includes a bit of history. Who lived in this land in ancient and more modern times? What were their lives like? What happened to them? What was it like when foreign cultures met and clashed?

The other sections will help you plan and arrange your trip. Find detailed directions in The Route. There is a sketch map for each day's hike along with recommendations for other maps to consult or bring with you. Information on public and private transport (taxis and shuttles) will help you to plan how to reach the trailhead and get back to your starting place when the hike is over.

Places to Stay lists locations and contact information for inns, bed-and-breakfasts, hotels, resorts, and hostels. This list may be partial if there are many lodging options. Prices are broken down into these categories:

LODGING COSTS

$ less than $100 | $$ $100-$150 | $$$ $150-$200 | $$$$ more than $200

Best of...

Every day's hike on this 200 mile walkabout brings surprises and delights: a pod of dolphin swimming along beside you, a lonely pocket beach beckoning you to stop for a swim, an unending beach all to yourself, a friendly inn from another era, a raucous tavern with a rock'n band and great fish tacos. Enjoy and savor at two miles an hour. Here are some of the best.

Best Coastal Bluff Preserves: Quiet sanctuaries of native plants, birds, and animals with spectacular views of the endless Pacific.

Point Dume (Exploring the Malibu Coast): This soaring ancient volcanic cone was a sacred spot to the Chumash and a landmark for 19th century sailors. Hike through fields of California poppies, giant coreopsis, and prickly pear cactus. Sea lions bark from rocky outcroppings at the foot of steep cliffs.

Dana Point Preserve (Newport Beach to San Clemente): Step back in time to the days before California's great cities were built and her shoreline became crowded with houses. Hummingbirds dart from flower to flower, mockingbirds serenade, and red-tailed hawks wheel above fields of cholla, bush sunflower, buckwheat, and fragrant sagebrush.

Torrey Pines State Reserve (Oceanside to La Jolla): Home of the rarest native pine tree in the Americas. Hike through forest and along 300 foot cliffs. Then descend to a perfect uninterrupted beach that stretches for miles.

Best endless beaches: Have you stood on a lonely beach that stretches to the horizon and felt a primal longing to hike, to find how far it goes, to explore that region where sea meets shore? Expect to have some of these long shorelines all to yourself.

San Onofre State Beach (San Clemente to Oceanside): Hike 5.5 miles of (almost) undeveloped beach. Stroll a few miles enjoying some of the best surfing you will see on the West Coast and past the out-of-place closed nuclear power plant. Then walk three miles of lonely pristine shoreline. Deeply eroded cliffs soar 150 feet to frame the beach. Savor the solitude with only shorebirds and harbor seals for companions.

Hotel del Coronado Dining

Torrey Pines State Beach (Oceanside to La Jolla): The three hundred foot sandstone escarpments of the state reserve protect one of the most isolated and serene beaches on the Southern California Coast. The state beach bleeds into Black's Beach and Torrey Pines City Beach. Millions live nearby, but you must be willing to hike to enjoy this grandeur.

Point Vicente

Silver Strand (La Jolla to Mexico): Hike eight miles on a narrow strip of sand that separates San Diego Bay from the Pacific. Beach lovers and kite surfers gather near the state park entrance, but snowy plover, marbled godwits, and you should have the rest of the shoreline to yourselves. Slow down and cherish a long walk on a beautiful beach.

Imperial Beach to the Border (La Jolla to Mexico): The estuary, marshland, and sand dunes of Border Field State Park flank this 6.6 mile round trip stretch of secluded beach. Pelicans, cormorants, gulls, egrets, terns, and plovers crowd the mouth of Tijuana River. You can wade across in the dry season and have the beach to yourself. Stroll to the border fence and greet Mexican families enjoying a day at the beach.

Best Patio Breakfasts – carbo loading for the trail: Here are a few of many great restaurants to start your day. There is so much more research to be done.

Uncle Bill's Pancake House, Manhattan Beach (Santa Monica to Santa Catalina): Bask in morning sunshine on the patio and relish delicious omelets and fluffy pancakes so large they spill over the sides of your plate. We passed through in October, and the special pumpkin pancakes were fabulous.

Sugar Shack, Huntington Beach (Santa Catalina to Newport Beach): Enjoy a hearty breakfast and friendly service at a sidewalk table while watching Huntington Beach slowly awaken.

Swami's Café, Encinitas (Oceanside to La Jolla): Across the street from the Self Realization Fellowship Retreat and Hermitage. Settle in on the veranda for omelets and home fries or try the acai bowl for an energizing shot of fruit and granola.

Best People Watching: Take a break from walking the shore and stroll paved paths and promenades that line the beaches of most coastal villages. The people watching will entertain and amuse you.

South Bay Bicycle Trail (Exploring the Malibu Coast and Santa Monica to Santa Catalina): Share this 22 mile esplanade with bicyclists, bikinied roller bladers, joggers, moms with babes in strollers, dog and power walkers. Tune into the boating life while strolling along the harbor of Marina del Rey. Pause to take in a beach volleyball game on Redondo Beach. Stop for a latte at an Hermosa Beach sidewalk café, and watch the world go by.

Venice Beach (Santa Monica to Santa Catalina): Grab a table at The Sidewalk Café and enjoy the festivities – skate dancers, body builders, street venders, aging hippies, young punks, artists, acrobats, and pan handlers accompanied by a steel drum band from the islands or an Andean flutist. The best show in town.

Ocean Front Walk, Pacific Beach (La Jolla to Mexico): Surfers and sun worshippers crowd the beach on summer days. Find a bench or pull up a chair at one of the bars or restaurants along Ocean Front Walk to watch the parade.

Best Peninsula Hiking: Separated from the dense urban life of L.A. and San Diego, two great promontories jut into the Pacific. Formed by the powerful forces of marine terracing and tectonic uplift, they invite a hiker to roam their rugged cliffs, cobblestone shores and beautiful beaches.

Palos Verdes Peninsula (Santa Monica to Santa Catalina): Hike narrow, rocky shores where waves crash on sculpted offshore shelves. Harbor seals, sea lions, dolphins, and shore birds may be your only companions. Then stroll a genteel trail on 200 foot cliffs

Crescent Bay

overlooking Santa Monica Bay, Santa Catalina Island, and the vast Pacific.

La Jolla Peninsula (Oceanside to La Jolla and La Jolla to Mexico): Snorkelers, long distance swimmers, stand up paddle boarders, and kayakers ply the clear waters of La Jolla Bay. From La Jolla Point, the long crescent shoreline arcs north to Palos Verdes Peninsula. To the south, hike along pocket beaches and crystalline lagoons where sea lions and harbor seals rest on offshore outcroppings.

Best old-time beach inns: Step back to a simpler time and spend a day or two at a motel out of the 50s or a beach house from another era.

Malibu Country Inn (Exploring the Malibu Coast): The place

to stay at Zuma Beach. Recently remodeled, it has kept the 1950s vibe of a Southern California beach motel. Rest up for the hike on your private deck and take a dip in the pool. Stroll down the road to Coral Beach Cantina, a popular roadhouse tucked under the trees. It shares outdoor seating with Zooma Sushi. Enjoy shrimp tempura with your carnitas.

Hiking Portuguese Cove

Zane Grey Pueblo Hotel, Avalon, Santa Catalina (Santa Monica to Santa Catalina and Santa Catalina to Newport Beach): Once the island home of the famed early twentieth century author of American West novels, it sits high on the hill overlooking Avalon Harbor. Mule deer wander off the slopes and through the patio surrounding the swimming pool. Affordable, funky, and charming.

Crystal Cove Park Historic District (Newport Beach to San Clemente): The state park and the Crystal Cove Alliance are remodeling ramshackle cottages from the 1930s – 1950s. Thirteen individual and three dorm-style cottages have been meticulously restored along the beach, on the bluffs, and up Los Trancos Canyon. It is a beautiful setting and a magical place to spend the night. Make your reservation early!

Del Mar Motel on the Beach (Oceanside to La Jolla): A throwback to 1970s Southern California motel design, it is nothing fancy, but step out of your room and onto the beach. They will provide you with beach towels, chairs, umbrellas, and boogie boards.

Best lodging splurges: After a few days on the trail, you may be ready for a luxurious respite.

Terranea Resort (Santa Monica to Santa Catalina): The only lodging on this section of Palos Verdes Coast, this is an expansive and opulent complex of condominiums, restaurants, and swimming pools perched on the edge of beautiful Long Point. Grab a beer at the poolside bar, immerse your weary body in the spa, and watch the sun set into the Pacific. Dine at one of the restaurants overlooking the ocean. Cap the evening with a stroll along coastal cliffs under a star filled sky. You will greet the morning happy and rested for the next day's hike.

The Inn on Mt. Ada, Avalon, Santa Catalina (Santa Monica to Santa Catalina and Santa Catalina to Newport Beach): William Wrigley Jr., the gum czar, bought the island of Santa Catalina in 1919 and built his mansion perched on the hill overlooking Avalon Bay. It is now a hotel where you can savor pampered luxury on the island of romance.

Crystal Pier Hotel and Cottages, Pacific Beach (La Jolla to Mexico): Restored 1930s style cottages line the private Crystal Pier with kitchenettes, living rooms, bedrooms, and private decks. It is said you can cast a line from your cottage window and catch dinner. Drift off to sleep soothed by the rhythm of the waves.

Hotel del Coronado, Coronado Village (La Jolla to Mexico): Built in 1888, it is one of the largest and oldest wooden structures in California. Sixteen presidents, from Benjamin Harrison to Barack Obama have been guests. Enjoy old world charm and a beautiful beach. The surrounding village has many inns, shops, bars with live music, and restaurants with sidewalk tables. Even if you don't stay at the hotel, visit its historic lobby, stroll the grounds, have a drink at the poolside bar, and hang out on the beach.

Best Hostels: Hostels are not just for youth anymore. Sleep in a dorm bed or a private room. Either way, you will have inexpensive lodging in a great setting with stimulating company from around the world.

Santa Monica Hostel (Exploring the Malibu Coast and Santa Monica to Santa Catalina): This is a prime location – two blocks from the beach and one from the nightlife of Santa Monica's Third Street Promenade. A friendly staff will greet you. They even throw in a complimentary breakfast.

Point Loma Hostel (La Jolla to Mexico): Small, intimate, and friendly, this hostel is a short walk from Ocean Beach on the way to Coronado.

Best lively coastal bar and restaurant scenes:

Santa Monica's Third Street Promenade (Exploring the Malibu Coast and Santa Monica to Santa Catalina): An auto-free pedestrian promenade just a few blocks from the pier. It is lively day and night – public art, street musicians, bars, restaurants, shops, and bookstores.

Avalon, Santa Catalina (Santa Monica to Santa Catalina and

Crystal Cove Cabin

Santa Catalina to Newport Beach): Relax and enjoy the slow island pace. Lounge in open air bars and restaurants along beautiful Avalon Harbor. Get your tiki bar fix at Luau Larry's with an (in) famous Wiki Wacker.

Looking North to Torrey Pines

Newport Beach Pier (Santa Catalina to Newport Beach, New-port Beach to San Clemente): The area around the Newport Pier has the feel of an old-time Southern California beach town. Cruise the many eateries and watering holes. Fans throng to multi-screen sports bars. Live music pours out of taverns and onto the street on balmy evenings any day of the week.

Best fish taco with a view: One could spend a lifetime seeking the perfect fish taco along this 200 mile walkabout.

Rockin' Baja Lobster, Newport Beach (Santa Catalina to New-port Beach, Newport Beach to San Clemente): Fortify yourself for the nightlife scene around the pier. The spicy ahi tacos are outra-geous.

Jose's Courtroom, La Jolla (Oceanside to La Jolla and La Jolla to Mexico): After a swim in La Jolla Cove, you can belly up to the sidewalk counter for a Corona and a plate of tacos. Gaze out to the ocean, and watch the world stroll by.

PB Shore Club, Pacific Beach (La Jolla to Mexico): Grab a bench seat along the second story open windows overlooking the beach. Enjoy the sunset and balmy sea breeze with a couple of heavenly lobster tacos.

Tin Fish Restaurant, Imperial Beach (La Jolla to Mexico): Take a long walk to the end of Imperial Beach Pier and feast on fish tacos and crab cakes while savoring views of the Pacific and the hills of Mexico.

Stay in Touch

The Walkabout California Community is growing, and there are so many more inn-to-inn hikes to be discovered in California. We continue to explore, and so do others. Come to *WalkaboutCalifornia.com.* Share your ideas about inn-to-inn hiking, your reviews of restaurants and inns that you enjoyed along the trail, your photos, and any questions about the hikes. Find out about new walkabouts. Share in the adventure of Walkabout California: Hiking Inn-to-Inn.

"Hark, now hear the sailors cry
smell the sea, and feel the sky
let your soul & spirit fly, into the mystic."

- Van Morrison, Into the Mystic

"Forget not that the earth delights to feel your bare feet and the winds long to play with your hair."

- *Khalil Gibran, The Prophet*

1. EXPLORING THE MALIBU COAST

"The Shallows –
A crane with legs wet
The sea cool"

- Matsuo Basho, The Narrow Road to the Deep North, 1689

View of
El Matador State Beach

THE MALIBU COAST, home to movie moguls and wealthy Angelinos, is a land of wild and extraordinary beauty waiting to be explored. Rugged, secluded beaches alternate with classic, expansive Southern California strands. Wildlife abounds – migrating whales, seabirds, seals, porpoises, and sea lions. The soaring Santa Monica Mountains form the backdrop. Because of rocky points that can only be passed at low tide, this is a demanding three day, 32 mile hike from Leo Carillo State Beach to the Santa Monica Pier. But the rewards are great - interesting inns, fine cuisine, and long days spent hiking and swimming in the wild Pacific. Experience the Southern California shore in a way that few have, hiking inn-to-inn on the Malibu Coast.

"The path of the heart takes you out of the mind."

- Ram Dass, One Liners

ITINERARY

DAY 1: Leo Carillo State Beach to Zuma County Beach		**7.9**
DAY 2: Zuma County Beach to Malibu Pier		**11.4**
DAY 3: Malibu Pier to Santa Monica Pier		**12.4**
TOTAL MILEAGE		**31.7**

Day 1: Leo Carrillo State Beach to Zuma County Beach

Start this walk at the north end of Los Angeles County, just south of
the Ventura County line, at Leo Carrillo State Beach, where Arroyo
Sequit Creek flows into the sea. It was mid-June when my wife,
Heidi, and I set out. The days were sunny and warm, and the ocean
beckoned us to swim several times each day. Although there was a
light morning fog at the state beach, families were already staking
out their territory for the day, lifeguards were on duty, and surfers
were riding three foot swells.

As you leave Leo Carrillo, the beach narrows, bordered by high
bluffs. Beyond them the rugged Santa Monica Mountains, dense
with chaparral, soar abruptly to the sky. The busy Pacific Coast
Highway is above the cliffs, but it cannot be seen or heard. The
wild beauty of the Pacific and its shoreline fills the senses.

Leo Carrillo to Point Zero

The California Coast runs east and west for most of this 32 mile walkabout. You'll hike secluded, unpopulated beaches, rocky points that require scrambling over boulders, narrow shores lined with lavish houses protected by riprap to slow the inevitable ero-

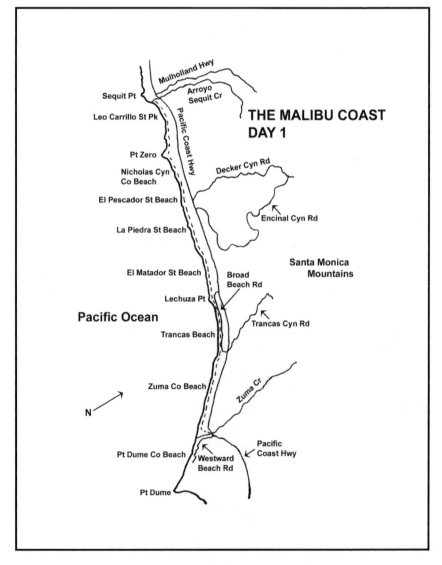

sion, and quintessential Southern California beaches attracting thousands of Angelinos.

With the exception of some very short sections, this walkabout can be hiked along the shoreline at low tide. Timing your hike with the tides is crucial. You can access tide charts at *http://tidesandcurrents.noaa.gov/tide_predictions.shtml.* In general you will find the best hiking conditions, wider beaches with firm sand, during the hours shortly before and after low tide.

Some rocky sections can only be passed when the tide is at its lowest. Please see The Route at the end of this chapter for the most difficult spots along with alternate trails. Pay attention to the frequent public paths and stairways. Private stairs can usually be identified by signs saying "PRIVATE PROPERTY" or "NO TRES-PASSING." If your path is blocked by the tide, you may want to wait for it to recede, or you can leave the shore and walk residential streets or the wide shoulder of Pacific Coast Highway until you can return to the beach. It helps to have footwear that gives you good traction over rocks and in the surf.

Hiking east from Leo Carrillo requires some bouldering, but the rocks are large and solid with good footing. Soon you are walking on the firm sand of a long arcing beach to Point Zero, the start of Nicolas Canyon County Beach and a favorite surfing spot. It is easily recognized by the lifeguard station perched on a bluff.

Take a diversion to the parkland above the beach and you will find an amazing Chumash Village recreated by the Wishtoyo Foundation. Domed houses made of tule reeds and willow branches are scattered on the hillside overlooking the Pacific along with a sweat lodge, ceremonial circle, and a *tomol* - a Chumash plank canoe. This walkabout hikes the southern range of Chumash lands, which stretched 200 miles north to Monterey County, east to San Joaquin

Chumash Village

Valley, and west to the Santa Barbara Channel Islands. A powerful and wealthy people, their population once totaled 18,000 to
20,000. They settled this territory more than 8,000 years ago.

In 1542, two Spanish ships, La Victoria and San Salvador, under
the command of Juan Rodriguez Cabrillo, set sail from Navidad,
Mexico. His mission was to explore the coast of New Spain and
to find a route to China. On October 10, after sailing into strong
headwinds from the north, the ships entered the relatively calm
waters of the Santa Barbara Channel and dropped anchor, perhaps
within sight of this modern Chumash village. Indian canoes quickly
left the shore. In each canoe, a dozen or so muscular men, clad
only with a waist string or a sea otter cloak, paddled and circled
the ships. They offered food and signs of friendship to the strange

visitors, who gratefully accepted. This was the first contact between the Chumash and Europeans.

Sailing north, Cabrillo and his crew saw many Chumash villages along coastal rivers and estuaries. Landing at present day Ventura, he claimed possession of the land for the Spanish Crown. *Diary of the Voyage*, thought to be written by Chief Pilot, Bartolome Ferrelo, chronicled their exploration of Chumash country.

> *"All these towns are between the first rancheria, Las Canoas, which they call Xucu, and this point (five miles west of Point Goleta). They are in a very good country with fine plains, and many groves and savannahs. The Indians go dressed in skins... and they wore their hair very long and tied up with long strings interwoven in the hair; to the strings they attached gewgaws of flint, bone, and wood...They say that in the interior there are many rancherias."*

It would be more than 200 years, in 1769, before the first European land expedition visited the Chumash. Led by Don Gaspar de Portolá, 62 men and almost 200 animals marched north from Mexico to establish Spain's claim on California. By the time the party reached the Chumash, they were near starvation. The Chumash greeted them with feasts of fish, game, and acorn mash. Traveling north, the expedition found large permanent villages, some with 100 houses and a 1,000 occupants. Father Juan Crespi chronicled their travels through Chumash lands.

> *"Ever since we first began meeting with houses laid out like towns, which was at Santa Catalina de Bononia, the villages have all been continuing to be this way, and the ones encountered are much more populous every day, with inhabitants living in regular towns with very good sized grass houses, round like half oranges, some of which are so large within that they must be able to lodge without hindrance sixty persons and more...*

They have their own kind of government, two, three, or four chiefs, and one of these chiefs is the headman, who gives orders to everyone."
— **August 20, 1769**

The waters of the Pacific are relatively peaceful south of Point Concepcion, where the coastline turns east, and the Channel Islands shelter the coast from raging winds out of the north and west. The Chumash were one of only two seafaring native California tribes. Their plank canoes, tomols, were finely crafted from redwood that drifted down from the north.

"These heathens are all very great fishermen who, as soon as day has broken, are at sea in their canoes catching their food. They have large fish traps very well made of rushes, gigs and hooks made from shell and bone, all very well made and stowed, and very good sized nets of different hues. This is entirely a very cultivated, quick, clever folk, skilled in everything, as is bespoken by the flint knives, very gorgeous, that they carry on their heads; the gorgeous and very elegant rushen baskets and bowls worthy of the admiration of any person of good taste; and the bowls made from wood and very shiny solid stone, so splendidly carven I do not know whether anyone using tools for the purpose could do better; whereas these people have no more than bone and flint to do it with. To this, add the canoes, so well made out of planking not two fingers thick, so smooth and so even – and they not possessing any saws or planes."
— **Father Juan Crespi, August 27, 1769**

Standing among the houses of the Wishtoyo Foundation's Chumash Village and looking out to the ocean, one can easily imagine what life might have been like only a few hundred years ago.

Our trail continues southeast on three state beaches: El Pesca-

La Piedra State Beach

dor, La Piedra, and El Matador. Rocky points jut out to separate them and this wildest section of the journey may require some scrambling. Houses can occasionally be spotted high on the cliffs between the state beaches and a few times they come down to the shore. Mostly you will find secluded beaches bordered by steep cliffs covered in coastal chaparral. Pelicans, gulls, and shore birds feed in the bountiful waters. Harbor seals rest on rocky outcroppings and swim just beyond breaking waves. The vast Pacific stretches to the horizon. Except for the forces of erosion and a few human staircases and paths, the state beaches protect a shoreline that has remained unchanged since this land was Chumash.

Shortly after El Matador State Beach you come to Lechuza Point at 5.1 miles where houses line the beach. This is the most difficult point to pass on the first day's hike, but getting around it on residential streets is quick and easy. Please see The Route for directions.

Trancas Beach lies beyond Lechuza Point. Houses line the shore on low bluffs reinforced by riprap - large boulders, some weighing more than a ton. Heavy plastic bags, six feet in diameter, filled with sand and stacked among the boulders, help to slow the relentless erosion. As we strolled, wading in the surf, a school of eight dolphins glided by, just outside the surf line, black dorsal fins cresting with each breath.

The final beach of the first day is Zuma County Beach. Long and expansive, it attracts hundreds of Angelinos to swim, surf, sunbathe, play volleyball, throw Frisbees, play fetch with their dogs, and simply enjoy a day at the shore. We found a spot and settled in to sunbathe, read, and people watch. What a joy it is to bask in the

Lechuza Point

Southern California sun and then to jump into the sea. We body-surfed and then floated beyond the breakers. What a relaxing way to end a beautiful day of hiking.

Stroll to the far end of the beach where Zuma Creek flows out of the mountains. Walk to the parking area and along the Pacific Coast Highway for a few hundred yards to the intersection of Westward Beach Road, where you will find the entrance to Malibu Country Inn.

The inn is a very comfortable, nicely refurbished 1950s style Southern California motel with a swimming pool. Rooms have private decks and larger suites have fireplaces. The Collection Restaurant and Bar is adjacent to the inn. You may want to dine at Coral Beach Cantina, a popular roadhouse tucked under the trees, a quarter mile south along the highway, which shares an outdoor dining space with Zooma Sushi. You can enjoy unagi with your chili verde.

There is a market in the small mall across the highway from Malibu Country Inn where you can buy supplies for tomorrow's lunch. It opens late in the morning, so you may want to shop the night before.

Day 2: Zuma County Beach to the Malibu Pier

Leaving Malibu Country Inn, walk Westward Beach Road to Point Dume County Beach. The road parallels the beach and becomes a long parking lot. Before you stands Point Dume, a towering ancient volcanic cone, 200 feet high, rising abruptly at the ocean's edge. You can hike the beach or stay on the pavement; they both end at the base of the point. A sandy stairstep trail starts at the end of the parking lot and climbs through coastal chaparral to the top. Trails are clearly marked with wire rope, protecting the fragile vegetation of this California state nature preserve. Prickly pear cactus bloom,

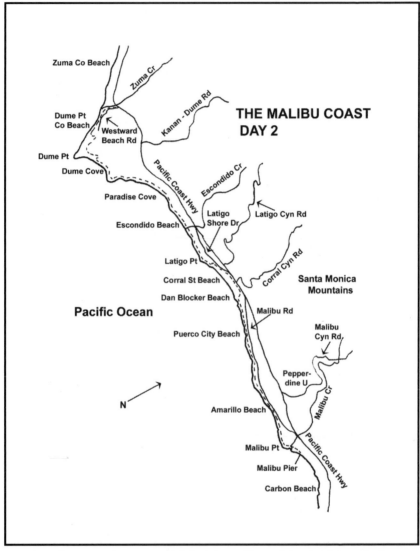

greeting the morning sun with bright yellow three inch petals forming a circular pattern. California poppies flourish in the sandy soil.
Giant coreopsis stand three feet tall with large clusters of yellow
daisy-like flowers. Keep right at the trail intersections, and follow
the path along the cliffs.

Dume Cove from Point Dume

A landmark for 19th century sailors, Point Dume was also considered a sacred place in the rich cosmology of the native Chumash. Their universe was made up of three worlds, each sitting on top of the other. We live in the middle world (*'Itiashup*), the "world of the people," a flat island surrounded by a great ocean. The middle world rests on two giant serpents that occasionally grow weary and need to move causing the world of the people to shake. The lower world (*C'oyinashup*) is the home of malevolent beings who can emerge into the middle world at night and cause harm to the people. The upper world (*'Alapay*) is the realm of the most powerful beings, the gods of the sun and the moon and the supernatural First People. The upper world rides the wings of a giant eagle that controls the movements of celestial bodies. The sweep of its wings determines the phases of the moon.

From the top of Point Dume, your eyes can follow the coastline northwest to Leo Carrillo State Beach and see your route from the first day. To the east lies Dume Cove, Malibu, and Santa Monica Bay extending to Palos Verdes peninsula. The trail skirts steep cliffs that plunge to the ocean. We watched cormorants resting on rocky outcroppings at the end of the point. Two kayakers fished, bobbing on gentle waves, and sea lions barked from rocks at the base of the cliffs. In the late winter and early spring, gray whales migrate from warm mating and calving lagoons in Baja California to rich feeding grounds in the Bering and Chukchi seas. Starting in February, mothers and their calves can easily be spotted as they pass in the shallow waters off the coast.

Stairs at the east end of the point descend to Dume Cove, a lovely protected beach. Mansions of the Malibu Riviera dot the

Point Dume County Beach

Paradise Cove

high cliffs. At 3.1 miles a rocky point forms the eastern end of the cove, which should be passable within a few hours of low tide.

At 4.1 miles you reach Paradise Cove, a privately run beach with a pier and restaurant, a nice place to stop for a late breakfast or early lunch. A small store has a selection of snacks for the trail.

Continue on narrow Escondido Beach, lined with houses on low bluffs. At its eastern end Latigo Point forms a rocky, challenging barrier that can be passed at low tide. If your passage is blocked, see The Route.

You will need to leave the beach shortly after Latigo Point. Houses block the far end of Corral State Beach. Take the unmarked public stairs at the end of a line of white condominiums with a blue roof, and hike the wide highway shoulder for 0.6 miles, the longest unavoidable stretch of highway hiking on this 32 mile walkabout.

Return to the shore at Dan Blocker Beach and continue on Puerco City Beach and then Amarillo Beach, two wide and lovely beaches lined with houses. You may be sharing these long strands with only the seabirds and ocean mammals that feed and lounge among offshore rocks. If passage becomes difficult, there are five public stairs that will take you to Malibu Road, a quiet residential lane that follows the coast.

Private interests have tried their best to deny public access to the shoreline along the Malibu Coast. You will see signs declaring "PRIVATE BEACH," an oxymoron. Access to the coast is every hiker's birthright. It is written into California state law that the coast is open to the public "seaward of the mean high tide line." If it is unsafe to walk below that line, you can legally walk above it. Home owners of Malibu Colony on the beautiful 0.6 mile beach before Malibu Point try desperately to discourage the public from using the public's beach. There is no stairway at the west end, but you can still access the beach. Look for a break in the houses near 24056 Malibu Road. Near a Coastal Conservancy sign that says "NO IMPROVED ACCESS," scramble down the boulders and stroll the beach.

A high fence that extends into the surf at the east end of the colony with a sign reading "PRIVATE BEACH" is built so that people can easily walk under, and is merely there to intimidate. Hiking the beaches of the Malibu Coast becomes a political act of asserting our right to coastal access.

Rounding Malibu Point you reach Malibu Lagoon and Surfrider Beach. The Lagoon meanders inland forming marshes and open water at the terminus of Malibu Creek. Flocks of pelicans, cormorants, ducks, coots, and night herons relax on the shore and in the

Surfrider Beach from Adamson House

calm waters.

A Chumash village of 1,000 souls named *Humaliwo*, meaning "the surf sounds loudly," once thrived on the shore of this creek and lagoon. Shortly after the 1769 Portolá expedition, the Spanish founded missions in Los Angeles, Ventura, and Santa Barbara. The Chumash had no immunity to European diseases, and the people were decimated by sickness and cruel Spanish rule.

Today's Malibu became part of a 13,000 acre 1802 land grant. Frederick Hastings Rindge purchased all of it in 1891, and his widow, Rhoda May, later fought to protect their land from outsiders. In 1929 Rhoda lost the battle and the Pacific Coast Highway was built. She subdivided and started to sell off lots.

In 1930, she and her new husband Merritt Adamson built Ad-

amson House on the eastern edge of the lagoon. This extraordinary
Spanish colonial revival house, famous for its beautiful tile work, is
open to the public and worth a visit. The house and grounds over-
look the beach and lagoon.

During the winter and spring, Malibu Creek flows to the sea. Its
egress is blocked during the dry season. Even when flowing, it is usually easy to wade across. If your passage is blocked, take the paths
along the lagoon to the parking lot, and walk into town along the
sidewalk. If you continue on the beach, you will find stairs at the far
end of Malibu Pier. You may want to stop at Beachcomber Café at
the base of the pier for happy hour before walking to your inn.

Malibu has only a few very pricey inns near the shore. The
Casa Malibu is right on the beach. At high tide the waves break
nearly on your patio. A continental breakfast of an apple and a
supermarket muffin wrapped in cellophane will send you off in the
morning.

Day 3: Malibu Pier to Santa Monica Pier

Heading east from the Malibu Pier, Carbon Beach forms a graceful arc. Houses line the beach cheek by jowl for the next six miles,
and there are few public stairs. Breaks in fences and some unfenced
embankments also offer exits from the beach if your way is blocked
by high tides.

Long beautiful beaches, separated by rocky points form the first
half of this day's hike. You will pass by perhaps the most expensive
real estate on the California Coast. Some of the fiercest battles to
maintain public access were fought over these beaches. David Gef-
fen, of DreamWorks fame, bought five adjacent parcels on Carbon
Beach in the 1980s including Doris Day's beach house. As part
of the permit to build his mansion, he agreed to provide a public
easement from the beach to the highway. He first ignored and then

fought that provision until he lost the final court battle in 2005. You will find the silver metal ramp next to his house a mile east of Malibu Pier.

This may be a good place to leave the beach and to hike the sidewalk and bike lane along Pacific Coast Highway. The shoreline hike from Carbon Beach to Las Tunas County Beach is beautiful and dramatic, but challenging.

If you do continue along the shore, round a rocky point at 1.8 miles that separates Carbon Beach from La Costa Beach. You may need to walk among the piers supporting beach houses and to climb over boulders in order to round this point if the tide is not low. You will reach Duke's Malibu Restaurant at 2.3 miles and Moonshadow Restaurant and Bar at 3.3 miles. We had to scramble over a twenty foot hill of boulders that protects Moonshadow from the

Malibu Beach and Pier

pounding surf. Diners were startled when we made our way over riprap just a few feet from their tables on the other side of picture windows. The food looked delicious.

Public stairs on Big Rock Beach allow you to get around the

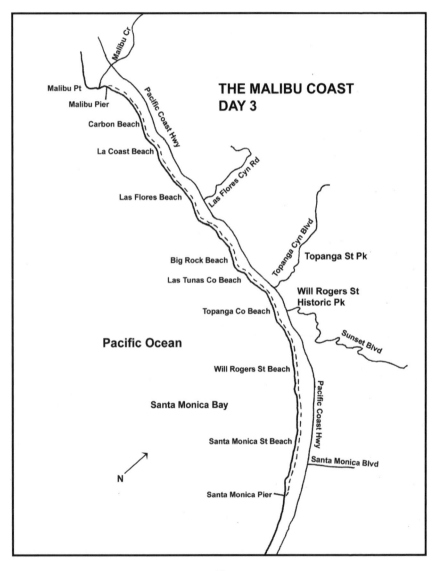

THE MALIBU COAST
DAY 3

Malibu Cr

Malibu Pt
Malibu Pier
Carbon Beach
La Coast Beach
Pacific Coast Hwy
Las Flores Beach
Las Flores Cyn Rd
Topanga Cyn Blvd
Big Rock Beach
Topanga St Pk
Las Tunas Co Beach
Will Rogers St Historic Pk
Topanga Co Beach
Sunset Blvd
Pacific Ocean
Will Rogers St Beach
Santa Monica Bay
Pacific Coast Hwy
Santa Monica St Beach
N
Santa Monica Blvd
Santa Monica Pier

Carbon Beach

point at the end of the beach if your way is blocked by the tide. After a short walk, another stairs just beyond the point drops down to Las Tunas County Beach.

At 6.1 miles you reach Topanga County Beach, a popular spot for swimming and a day at the shore. You might want to visit the Cholata Thai Restaurant, across the highway. We ordered take out and enjoyed a delicious lunch on the beach.

The journey now changes dramatically to easy hiking on broad beaches. You will see a sign for the L.A. city limits at 7.4 miles. The coastline turns southeast, and here begins miles of uninterrupted wide, classic Southern California beaches starting with Will Rogers State Beach and then Santa Monica State Beach. You can see the ferris wheel on Santa Monica Pier, five miles down the coast.

The South Bay Bicycle Trail starts at 9.5 miles. This paved path snakes twenty two miles along the beaches all the way to Torrance. Hike along the water's edge or stroll the path. Either way is a celebration of Southern California beach life – surfing, volleyball, swimming, sunbathing, Frisbees, rollerblading, kites, bikes, dogs, and body surfing. Enjoy the delights that the Santa Monica shore has to offer, the tacky pleasures of Santa Monica Pier, or the plentiful bars and restaurants on Third Street Promenade.

The Malibu Coast is wild and beautiful, a treasure of bountiful sea life, rugged coastline, exquisite beaches, and towering mountains. Private property makes much of it seem inaccessible, but it is ours to explore and enjoy, and what better way than leaving the car behind and taking a walkabout on the Malibu Coast.

THE ROUTE

This Walkabout begins at Leo Carrillo State Beach near the Ventura and Los Angeles county line. All of the 32 mile journey, with the exception of some very short sections, can be hiked along the shoreline at low tide. Tide schedules are available at *http://tidesand-currents.noaa.gov/tide_predictions.shtm.* The hours before and after low tide are also the times when you will find the best hiking conditions - wider beaches with firm sand.

You will find long, beautiful beaches separated by rocky points. Pay attention to the frequent public paths and stairways that lead up from the shore. Private stairs can usually be identified by signs reading "PRIVATE PROPERTY" or "NO TRESPASSING." Each state and county beach has a public path or stairway leading to the Pacific Coast Highway. If your way is blocked, wait for the tide to recede, or leave the beach and walk residential streets or the wide shoulder of the highway until you can return to the shore.

All mileages listed for a given day are cumulative.

Day 1: Leo Carrillo State Beach to Zuma County Beach

Enter Leo Carrillo State Beach by car on the north side of the Pacific Coast Highway. Lechuza Point at 5.1 miles is the most difficult spot to pass if the tide is not at its lowest.
Tip: Start hiking 2 to 2.5 hours before low tide.

Leo Carrillo State Beach to Nicholas Canyon County Beach **1.5 miles**
To El Pescador State Beach..**2.6 miles**
To La Piedra State Beach ....**3.2 miles**
To El Matador State Beach ....**4.0 miles**

Houses line the beach at the east end of El Matador. You may need to climb over riprap to reach Lechuza Point. ....**5.1 miles**

Chumash Tomol

Lechuza Point is easily recognized because houses line the beach. If you cannot round the point along the shore, take the private road (open to walkers) that comes down to the beach. Stroll up the road and exit through the iron door to the right of the gate onto Broad Beach Rd. Turn right and walk a quarter mile to the public stairs at 31345 Broad Beach Rd. to Trancas Beach. ....**6.2 miles**

To the east end of Zuma County Beach ....**total miles: 7.9**

Zuma Beach ends and Point Dume County Beach begins at Zuma Creek. Walk the shoulder of the Pacific Coast Highway for a few hundred yards to the intersection of Westward Beach Rd. and find the entrance to Malibu Country Inn.

Day 2: Zuma County Beach to Malibu Pier

Latigo Point at 6.1 miles is the most difficult spot to pass on this leg, so it is best to start hiking approximately three hours before low tide. Take Westward Beach Rd. to Point Dume County Beach. The road follows the beach, becomes a parking lot, and ends at the base of Point Dume. Zuma Beach to base of Point Dume ....**1.5 miles**

Ascend the sandy path at the end of the parking lot up Point Dume. Stay right and follow the trail past the lookout to a staircase descending to Dume Cove. ....**2.7 miles**

To Paradise Cove pier ....**4.1 miles**

After Paradise Cove, you'll reach Escondido Beach. To Latigo Point ....**6.1 miles**

If your passage is blocked at Latigo Point, return to the stairs just before Escondido Creek, walk briefly on the shoulder of the Pacific Coast Highway for a short distance to Latigo Shore Dr. Take this quiet lane until it returns to the highway. Walk the highway shoulder for another 0.6 miles to reach Dan Blocker Beach. If you can walk around Latigo Point, you'll reach Corral State Beach ....**6.5 miles**

Adamson House Tile Work

Two houses at the east end of Corral State Beach block the way. Take the stairs at the far end of a line of white condos with a blue roof to Latigo Shore Dr. Turn right and hike the wide shoulder of Pacific Coast Highway to Dan Blocker Beach. This 0.6 mile stretch is the longest mandatory section of road hiking on this walkabout.
To Dan Blocker Beach ....**7.1 miles**

The highway turns inland. A sandy path leads up to the start of Malibu Road, which parallels the shore. ....**8.1 miles**

Hike Puerco City Beach to Amarillo Beach. A rocky point separates the two beaches and passage can be tricky. There are five stairways along the two beaches leading to Malibu Rd.
To Amarillo Beach ....**9.9 miles**

The 0.6 mile beach to Malibu Point can be accessed by scrambling

Puerco City Beach

down boulders at a break in the houses near 24056 Malibu Rd. at a Coastal Conservancy "NO IMPROVED ACCESS" sign. To Malibu Point ....**11.0 miles**

Malibu Creek forms the Malibu Lagoon and flows into the Pacific at Surfrider Beach. It can usually be waded, but if your path is blocked, take one of the lagoon trails to the highway for a short walk to the Malibu Pier. .... **total miles 11.4** The stairs are at the far side of the pier.

Day 3: Malibu Pier to Santa Monica Pier

The first half of this hike requires some scrambling over rocks, but you'll hike wide easy beaches on the second half. Big Rock Beach at 3.8 miles and Las Tunas County Beach at 5.2 miles are the most difficult spots to pass on this leg. You may want to start hiking two hours before low tide. If your passage is blocked, return to the nearest access to Pacific Coast Hwy. Walk the sidewalk or bike lane until you can return to the shore. You can avoid the challenging sections all together by leaving Carbon Beach on a public access ramp 1.0 mile from Malibu Pier and hiking on the sidewalk or bike lane to Las Tunas County Beach.

Malibu Pier to the east end of Carbon Beach .... **1.8 miles**

To Las Flores Beach .... **2.6 miles**

To Big Rock Beach... **3.8 miles**

The point at the end of Big Rock Beach may be difficult to pass. You will find stairs shortly before and after the point. The first stairs are found shortly after the Moonshadow Restaurant. To Las Tunas County Beach... **5.2 miles**

Malibu Pier

To Topanga County Beach..**6.1 miles**

Stroll wide beaches to the Santa Monica Pier. Two buildings between Topanga County Beach and Will Rogers State Beach block a clear passage and require short exits from the shore. To Will Rogers State Beach..**7.4 miles**

To South Bay Bicycle Trail...**9.5 miles**

Hikers, skaters, strollers, and bicyclists enjoy this twenty mile paved path. You may want to continue along the beach or take the path to Santa Monica Pier...**total miles 12.4**

TRANSPORTATION

Public Transportation to Leo Carrillo State Beach from Santa Monica

Traveling to Leo Carrillo State Beach from Santa Monica by public transportation is a painless two-step process. An L.A. County Metro bus will take you most of the way. Visit *www.metro.net* for easy trip planning. Catch Metro Bus 534 on Ocean Ave. at Colorado Ave. The bus stop is on the west side of Ocean Ave., a bit counter intuitive because you start out heading south, but the bus quickly makes a U-turn onto Pacific Coast Highway and speeds north making only a few stops until Malibu. It passes Zuma County Beach and ends at the corner of Trancas Canyon Rd. and the Pacific Coast Highway. You will need to take a taxi for the final 6 miles. Call Yellow Cab 310-456-5303 or Malibu Yellow Cab 310-456-0500. The fare to Leo Carrillo is around $20.

Flying into Los Angeles

Take a Super Shuttle van from Los Angeles International Airport to Santa Monica for $15 per person. For information and reservations call 800-258-3826 or try *www.supershuttle.com.* Super Shuttle also serves other L.A. area airports.

MAPS

The U.S. Geological Survey sells topographical hiking maps and provides free maps you can download. Visit *http://store.usgs.gov* and go to the map locator.

• Triunfo Pass – Leo Carrillo State Beach to El Matador State Beach
• Point Dume – El Matador State Beach to Corral State Beach
• Malibu Beach – Corral State Beach to Big Rock Beach
• Topanga – Big Rock Beach to Santa Monica State Beach

PLACES TO STAY

LODGING COSTS

$ less than $100 | $$ $100-$150 | $$$ $150-$200 | $$$$ more than $200

Zuma County Beach

Malibu Country Inn
6506 Westward Beach Road
310-457-9622
www.Malibucountryinn.com
$$$-$$$$
Swimming pool

Malibu

These inns are walking distance from Malibu Pier

Malibu Beach Inn
22878 Pacific Coast Hwy.
310 456-6444
www.malibubeachinn.com
$$$$

Casa Malibu Inn
22752 Pacific Coast Hwy.
310-456-2219
800-831-0858
$$$$

Malibu Motel
22541 Pacific Coast Hwy.
310-456-6169
www.themalibumotel.com
$$ - $$$$

Santa Monica

These inns are a short walk from Santa Monica Pier

Santa Monica Hostel
1436 2nd St.
310- 393-9913
www.hilosangeles.org
$
Great location
Singles from $30 per night
Continental breakfast

Georgian Hotel
1415 Ocean Ave.
310- 395-9945
www.georgianhotel.com
$$$$

Doubletree Santa Monica
1707 4th St.
310- 395-3332
www.doubletree.com
$$$ - $$$$

Hotel Casa Del Mar
1910 Ocean Way
(310) 581-5533
www.hotelcasadelmar.com
$$$$

The Huntley Hotel
1111 2nd St.
310- 394-5454
www.thehuntleyhotel.com
$$$$

Ocean View Hotel
1447 Ocean Ave.
800-452-4888
www.oceanviewsantamonica.com
$$-$$$

Notes

2. Santa Monica to Santa Catalina

"Walking takes longer...than any other known form of locomotion except crawling. Thus it stretches time and prolongs life. Life is already too short to waste on speed."

- Edward Abbey, Walking

*View of
Point Vicente*

THIS MODERATE THREE-DAY, 38 mile adventure hikes a Pacific shoreline that varies from wide Southern California swimming beaches, to paths along coastal bluffs, to boulder hopping under steep cliffs where few hikers venture. It passes through sections of deep urban development as well as untouched wilderness where your only company will be sea mammals and shore birds. Along the way you'll visit delightful beach towns, a luxurious resort, and the beautiful island of Santa Catalina.

> *"Earth and sky, woods and fields, lakes and rivers, the mountain and the sea, are excellent schoolmasters, and teach some of us more than we can ever learn from books."*
>
> *- John Lubbock, The Use of Life*

ITINERARY

DAY 1:	Santa Monica to Manhattan Beach	**12.4**
DAY 2:	Manhattan Beach to Long Point, Palos Verdes Peninsula	**13.3**
DAY 3:	Long Point to San Pedro Ferry Terminal to Santa Catalina	**12.3**
TOTAL MILEAGE		**38.0**

This is an extraordinarily varied walkabout, a hike through diverse terrain and cultures. It seems fitting that the first stretch leaves Santa Monica Pier and plunges into the exotic world of Venice Beach. You may want to walk the paved promenade rather than the shoreline on the first 2.7 miles of this walkabout, and experience a unique beach community.

My friend Scott and I strolled the Venice Boardwalk on a warm October evening before we started hiking. It did not disappoint. A steady flow of tourists and locals walked and watched skate dancers; steroidal bodybuilders; and intense games of volleyball, paddle tennis, handball, and basketball. Street venders hawked t-shirts, hats, incense, used books, jewelry, macramé, pipes, sunglasses, henna tattoos, and medical marijuana certificates. We settled in for happy hour at perhaps the best spot for people watching - The Sidewalk Café. It was like the circus with beer, starring bikini roller-bladers, aging hippies, young punks, orthodox Jews, artists, musicians, and panhandlers. The lilting rhythms of a steel drum band played background music, and the air was flavored with the fragrance of incense and marijuana.

Do you need a book for the trail? Stop next door, away from the clamor, and into the landmark Small World Books. You'll find the latest releases, classics, and the works of local authors and small presses.

Day 1: Santa Monica Pier to Manhattan Beach

Leaving Santa Monica, our trail follows the South Bay Bicycle Path for the first day and a half, a total of 17.9 miles. You can walk the paved bike path or enjoy a stroll on the beach. There are two spots where you'll need to leave the shore to pass around harbors. The first turn inland comes at Venice Pier to hike around Marina del Rey, the world's largest man-made harbor devoted to small craft. Nineteen marinas are home for 6,500 boats. Please see The Route for detailed directions.

The harbor was dredged from salt marshes fed by Bollona Creek. After rounding Marina del Rey, our trail follows the creek back to the beach. When the Spanish first settled in Los Angeles basin, the course of the L.A. River turned west near present day Bunker Hill, merging with Ballona Creek and flowing into Santa Monica Bay. But furious storms pounded Southern California in the winter of 1824 and 1825 causing great floods. Settlers had never seen such high water. The L.A. River jumped its banks careened though littoral lowlands, and forged a new sinuous course through the vast alluvial plain. Eventually swinging around Palos Verdes

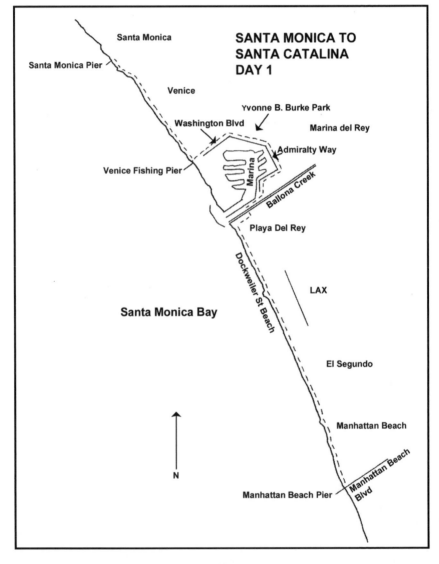

SANTA MONICA TO
SANTA CATALINA
DAY 1

Santa Monica

Santa Monica Pier

Venice

Yvonne B. Burke Park

Washington Blvd

Marina del Rey

Admiralty Way

Venice Fishing Pier

Marina

Ballona Creek

Playa Del Rey

Dockweiler St Beach

LAX

Santa Monica Bay

El Segundo

Manhattan Beach

N

Manhattan Beach Blvd

Manhattan Beach Pier

South Bay Bicycle Path

Peninsula, the L.A. River found its current exit to the Pacific eleven miles south in San Pedro Bay. Ballona Creek continues to flow into Santa Monica Bay. It is now tamed, mostly hemmed in by paved canals.

Our trail returns to the beach at Playa del Rey and Dockweiler State Beach. This is the most industrial section of coastline along the entire 200 miles of our Southern California Coast Walkabout. You will pass under the flight path of LAX and by a massive sewage treatment plant. On your left is crude urban development, on your right, a beautiful beach and the wild Pacific. The sound of crashing waves is interrupted every 4-5 minutes by the roar of jets.

Docweiller State Beach

We shared the beach with only a few joggers and scores of birds. Flocks of avocets, gulls, sandpipers, and curlews grazed and rested along the shore. A freighter had prematurely unloaded its cargo of tennis balls. Hundreds floated in the surf and scattered on the beach. We played tennis ball soccer and went out for passes until we left the industrial zone and strolled onto serene and inviting Manhattan Beach.

This begins a ten-mile stretch of classic Southern California beaches and fun beach towns that have delighted Angelinos for decades – Manhattan, Hermosa, and Redondo. Even in October, the water was great for swimming, warmed by a long summer. Surfers crowded the waves around Manhattan Beach Municipal Pier.

Enjoy the bustle of Manhattan Beach's commercial district with its many restaurants and bars by walking a few blocks inland from the pier. This is a great spot for a rest day to savor the joys of the

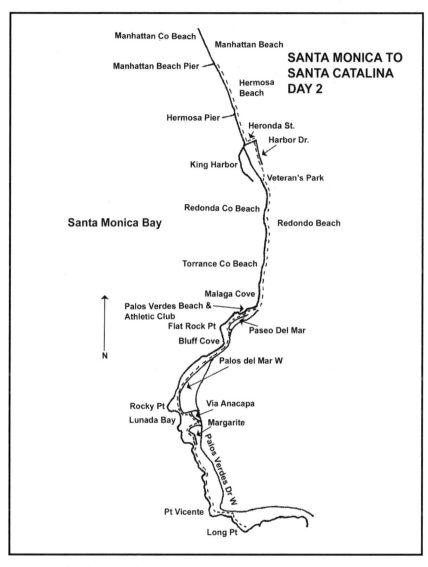

ocean and a fun beach town.

Day 2:
Manhattan Beach to Long Point, Palos Verdes Peninsula

Stop at Uncle Bill's Pancake House for a mouthwatering breakfast

Manhattan Beach

to start this hiking day. Just three blocks inland from the pier and a few blocks north at 13th and Highland, it has been a Manhattan Beach favorite for fifty years. Bask in morning sunshine on the patio and enjoy delicious omelets and fluffy pancakes so large they spill over the sides of the plate.

Our waitress, Maria, told us, "The U.S. is the land of pancakes. I have traveled all over – to Oregon and Washington, to Canada, to the East Coast. These are the best." On the October morning of our journey, they featured special pumpkin pancakes.

The next five and a half miles will enchant Southern California beach lovers. Starting at Manhattan Beach, walk the shoreline or take the bike path. Both are fun. The shoreline takes you along some of the most beautiful swimming beaches in the state. The bike path is lined with colorful beach houses. It will entertain you with bikers, joggers, roller bladers, mothers with babes in strollers, and fellow walkers.

Hermosa Beach offers restaurants and coffee shops on the promenade just inland from the municipal pier. Take a break, and watch competitive beach volleyball.

Our trail jogs inland to get around the marina at King Har-

Hermosa Beach Volleyball

bor. It returns to the shore at Redondo Beach. Manhattan Beach, Hermosa Beach and Redondo Beach are all residential beach towns where the focus and attraction is the Pacific. Continue to Torrance County Beach. The center of Torrance is a few miles inland, but the beach is beautiful.

The 22 mile South Bay Bicycle Trail ends at Torrance, but our beach walk continues for another mile where it stops abruptly at the rising hills and steep cliffs of Palos Verdes Peninsula. The hike changes from sandy beach to rugged boulder strewn shoreline and soaring bluffs.

You may choose between two routes when you reach the end of the beach. Please see The Route. The shoreline route is magnificent but challenging, a scramble over boulders and cobblestones under steep cliffs. It can be hiked when the tide is low and the weather mild. Check tide tables at *http://tidesandcurrents.noaa.gov/tide_predictions.shtml.* This more adventurous route brings you close to raw nature with the waves of the Pacific crashing on a narrow rocky shore. Harbor seals, sea lions, dolphins, and shorebirds will probably be your only companions. Hike around Flat Rock Point where a path leads up to the bluffs or continue around Bluff Cove and along Palos Verdes Estates Shoreline Preserve to Lunada Bay,

Malaga Cove

and take the path to the bluffs.

The more genteel Bluff Route leaves the shore at the end of the beach and climbs a paved driveway above Palos Verdes Beach and Athletic Club and their pristine pool on cliffs above the rugged

Terranea

coast. Reaching the top of 200 foot bluffs, the view is spectacular. Santa Monica Bay arcs north to Malibu. To the west, the island of Santa Catalina pierces the blue Pacific.

Hike the bluffs alternating between residential streets and open space along the cliffs. The neighborhoods of Palos Verdes Estates have palatial Mediterranean style houses reminiscent of the estates of Roman aristocracy on the coast of Italy.

Follow winding Seascape Trail along cliffs to Point Vicente. The steep escarpment plunging to crashing waves is breathtaking, and every turn of the trail brings new dazzling views.

Point Vicente Lighthouse stands on a rugged promontory surrounded by a grassy park. Built in 1926, its light still shines, guiding ships and pleasure craft, and warning them to steer clear of treacherous rocks. Visit the interpretive center for interesting exhibits on the history of the peninsula.

The park is one of the best places on the coast for viewing gray whales on their annual 12,000 mile migration. Leaving their Artic feeding grounds in the cold waters of Alaska and the Bering Sea, they swim south to the warm lagoons of Baja California. Around 15,000 of these magnificent giants head south from mid-December through February. You can see them spouting in a series of 3-5 breaths in 15-30 second intervals. Then raising their flukes, they dive for 3-5 minutes. In the spring, they return with newborn calves for the northward journey, this time at a slower pace and closer to shore.

Leaving the park, walk a mile along bluffs to Terranea Resort, the only lodging on this section of Palos Verdes Coast. It is an expansive, opulent, pretentious complex of condominiums, restaurants, swimming pools, a fitness center, and golf course perched on the edge of beautiful Long Point. It has exquisitely manicured grounds and alluring paths along rugged cliffs. Enjoy a well-earned respite in pampered luxury.

The rooms are spacious with verandas opening to courtyards and gardens. Savor a soak in your posh bathroom's tub and enjoy luxurious lotions, shampoos, bath salts, and gels. Stop at the bar and grab a beer to take to the vast swimming pool and spa where you can immerse your weary body and watch the sun set into the Pacific. Then dine at one of the many restaurants with views of the ocean. Cap the evening with a stroll along the cliffs under a star filled sky. You will be ready in the morning for the final day's hike.

Day 3:
Long Point, Palos Verdes Peninsula to San Pedro Ferry Terminal and Santa Catalina

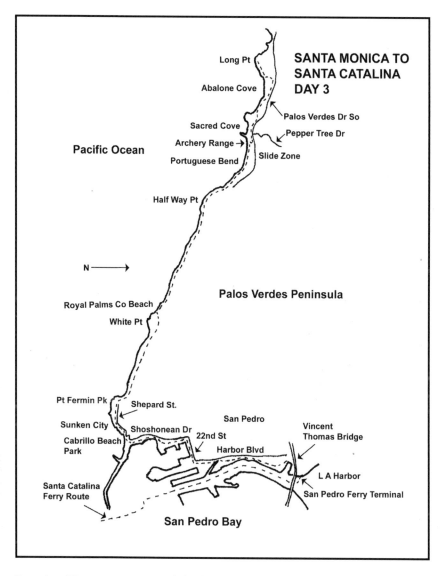

SANTA MONICA TO
SANTA CATALINA
DAY 3

Long Pt

Abalone Cove

Palos Verdes Dr So

Sacred Cove

Pepper Tree Dr

Archery Range →

Portuguese Bend

Slide Zone

Pacific Ocean

Half Way Pt

N ⟶

Palos Verdes Peninsula

Royal Palms Co Beach

White Pt

Pt Fermin Pk

Shepard St.

San Pedro

Vincent
Thomas Bridge

Sunken City

Shoshonean Dr

Cabrillo Beach
Park

22nd St

Harbor Blvd

Santa Catalina
Ferry Route

L A Harbor

San Pedro Ferry Terminal

San Pedro Bay

Leaving Terranea Resort, hike bluff trails and residential streets to
Abalone Cove. The crescent bay invites you to visit its long sandy
beach. Portuguese Point forms the far boundary of the cove. Its
cliffs rise 200 feet above the shore, and as the tide recedes, a newly

Abalone Cove

formed marine terrace is revealed, exposing tide pools to be explored.

Marine terraces are at the heart of the geological story of Palos Verdes Peninsula. Once submerged under the Pacific, powerful planetary forces raised it from the sea. Thin plates of the earth's crust, floating on an ocean of semi-fluid mantle, collide at California's western edge creating uplift. Millions of years ago, an island emerged. Waves of the ancient ocean leveled the sea floor creating terraces, and the island continued to rise. Coastal mountains eroded, and rivers deposited alluvial soil in the marine basin west of the island, eventually connecting it to the continent.

Uplift and marine terracing continues today. Palos Verdes' coastal bluffs are the latest terrace to emerge. Thirteen major terraces form the peninsula, climbing to San Pedro Hill at 1,480 feet.

Stroll the bluffs of Abalone Cove Shoreline Park, and follow The Route to a gravel road that descends to the sea. Enter the amazing Portuguese Bend Slide Zone, one of the earth's oldest active landslides.

In the summer of 1956, neighbors above Portuguese Bend were stunned when a waterline ruptured and their houses started to shift. It quickly became clear that this was not a one-time event. Crevasses suddenly opened in their lawns. The walls of their houses separated and buckled. Ceilings collapsed. The land was moving six inches a day, sliding toward the sea.

Portuguese Bend

The landslide has slowed to less than an inch a day, but large sections of earth periodically separate and crumble. Palos Verdes Drive South has been rebuilt again and again.

Descending the gravel road to an archery range, you will pass two abandoned houses perched on the slope at odd angles. They once sat firmly above the roadway. Then they slid downhill and

Hiking Portuguese Cove

now rest below it. The land around is jumbled and unstable.

It was here that I made a mistake. We weren't sure whether to continue on the gravel road or to make a beeline to the coast. I decided to hike cross-country to the bluffs, only a few hundred yards, to scout our route. Forty feet in I hit unstable land. It opened below me, and I fell into a crevasse to my chest, catching myself with my elbows. Scott rushed to help pull me out, but it wasn't easy. There was no firm ground. It kept crumbling. Eventually, he got me out and on more stable ground. We carefully made our way back to the gravel road.

Stay on the road through the archery range, and take the path that descends to a small beach, leaving civilization and entering the world of the wild, untamed Pacific Coast. Hike the shoreline for the next 3.4 miles along pretty beaches and rocky shore.

Your pace slows as you must walk mindfully over boulders and cobblestones. Your focus leaves the world of roads and structures and turns to the power of the Pacific. Gulls, brown pelicans, and cormorants fish just offshore. Pelicans dive, beaks piercing the surface. Screeching gulls swarm in, hoping to pick up leftover morsels. The shore is littered with detritus of the slide zone – sections of chain-link fence, water pipes, and chunks of asphalt litter the rocky shore.

This is Portuguese Bend, a long cove where Portuguese whalers hunted gray whales from shore in the mid-1800s. It was a danger-

Royal Palms County Beach

ous and lucrative business. A lookout manned the bluffs watching for whales. When spotted, he gave a shout and pointed his flag toward the prey. Boats were launched and rowed within striking distance. Gunners took aim and fired an exploding harpoon. It would often require more than one wound to kill the massive mammal. Boats were sometimes destroyed by a blow from the fluke of a furious whale.

The catch was towed to shore to be processed. Great kettles rested on fires cooking fat and blubber to render the precious oil.

Times have changed. A beach club now sits on a sandy section of the cove with tennis courts, palapas, and picnic tables. Beyond the club, the broad beach turns rocky again with smooth cobblestones. Visitors have laid out stone labyrinths on the flat beach.

Rounding the base of Portuguese Bend, explore the tide pools alive with mollusks, sea stars, urchins, and anemones. Continue along the rocky shoreline to Royal Palms County Beach, a pretty pair of coves bordered with rows of palm trees. A paved picnic area sits a few feet above the pounding sea. This was the site of White Point Hot Springs Hotel, a popular beach resort in the 1920s and 30s. Guests danced the Charleston on this veranda turned picnic area. Old stone fireplaces are all that remain of a 50 room hotel, cabins, and a pier. Hot sulfur springs fed large swimming pools. The Long Beach earthquake of 1933 shut off the flow from the springs, and fierce storms damaged the hotel. Eventually, the Great Depression and the onset of World War II forced its closure.

Return to the bluffs and stroll to Point Fermin Park, a grassy promontory with stately magnolias, perched on the southeast edge of Palos Verdes Peninsula. We have been hiking the coast of the City of Angels for three days, and this is its southernmost tip. The coast turns north here to form San Pedro Bay, the entrance to Long Beach and L.A. harbors. Cruise ships and massive freighters steam in and out of channels. Wind and kite surfers scream across the bay's wide mouth.

You have hiked Palos Verdes Peninsula. Many travel its roads

Avalon Bay Santa Catalina

every day, but few experience its rugged shores. This is an amazing section of California's coast - not an easy hike, but a wild and enchanted land.

Sunken City sits at the end of the park. Once a community of orderly bungalows, it started to slide one morning in 1929. Soon the ground was shifting a foot a day. Most of the houses were saved and moved. Sunken City was abandoned. Today it is an eerie ghost town of broken sidewalks, uprooted trees, streets to nowhere, and eroded cliffs sliding to the sea.

Walker Café, next to the park, beckons the hiker to pay a visit. A dilapidated structure with an ancient, barely readable sign, it caters to a friendly motorcycle crowd. The menu and prices are straight out of the fifties, the atmosphere congenial and neighborly.

Sunken City

Stop here and fuel up for the final leg through San Pedro.

Follow The Route through the neighborhoods of San Pedro above the coast and along the marina. Stay overnight or walk to the Catalina Ferry Terminal. Either way, stop to visit the bars and restaurants along the wharf where you can order large treys of shrimp or calamari, sit on the wharf, and watch the ships – from small sailboats to colossal freighters – sail by.

Santa Catalina

Treat yourself to a day or two on the island of Santa Catalina. The ferry ride from San Pedro takes an hour. Make reservations at *www.catalinaexpress.com*. When you disembark at Avalon's deep blue harbor crowded with sailboats, it feels as though you have taken a time machine to another land and era. The pace is slow.

The most popular vehicles are golf carts.

Stroll the town and the surrounding hills, rent a kayak and explore the coastline, snorkel in the kelp forest of Lovers Cove, pump up your adrenaline on the zip line that descends from mountain top to sea, enjoy the restaurants and bars along the waterfront, or just relax. You are on island time.

THE ROUTE

Sections of days 2 and 3 of this 38 mile adventure are best hiked when the tide is not high. Tide schedules are available at *http://tidesandcurrents.noaa.gov/tide_predictions.shtm*. The hours before and after low tide are also best for hiking with wider beaches and firm sand.

Rodondo Beach

All mileages listed for a given day are cumulative.

Day 1: Santa Monica Pier to Manhattan Beach

Leaving Santa Monica Pier, hike south along the shore or paved promenade to Venice Pier...**2.7 miles**

Turn inland at Venice Pier on Washington Blvd. for the walk around Marina del Rey. Look for Mildred Ave. on the left. This is where you turn right on the bike path through Yvonne B. Burke Park...**4.1 miles**

Follow the bike path across Admiralty Way and through the library parking lot. Continue on the bike path, turning right on Fiji Way, which ends at the U.S. Coast Guard Station. The path keeps going to the Ballona Creek channel. Turn right, stroll along the creek, cross the bridge, and return to the beach..**6.5 miles**

Manhattan Beach Pier

Ballona Creek

Hike the beach or the paved bike path to Manhattan Beach Municipal Pier...**total miles 12.4**

Day 2:
Manhattan Beach to Long Point, Palos Verdes Peninsula

Hike the beach or bike path to Hermosa Beach Municipal Pier.
.... **1.6 miles**

Continue to King Harbor where the beach ends and the bike path turns inland. ....**2.3 miles**

Walk on Herondo St. Turn right on Harbor Dr. until it ends. Continue on the bike path through the ground floor of a parking structure into Veteran's Park where you can return to the shore at Redondo Beach.
....**3.6 miles**

To Torrance Co. Beach and the end of the South Bay Bicycle Trail.
....**5.5 miles**

Continue along the beach until it ends at Malaga Cove ......**6.4 miles**

From Malaga Cove you can take the Shoreline Route or the Bluff Route.

Bluff Route: Take the paved road from the beach to the bluffs. The road goes above the Palos Verdes Beach and Athletic Club. Turn right on Paseo Del Mar until it ends at Palos Verdes Dr. West and turn right.
....**7.4 miles**

Bare right on Paseo Del Mar West. Turn right on Via Anacapa. Turn right on Palos Verdes Dr. West for 100 yards, and right on Margarite until it ends. Pass through the gate, and follow Seascape Trail along the bluffs to Point Vicente...**12.4 miles**

Shoreline Route: This route follows the shore beyond Malaga Cove. It is a challenging trail, hiking over rocky beaches and boulders. It should only be attempted at low tide. For tide tables, go to *http://tidesandcurrents.noaa.gov/tide_predictions.shtml.* There is a path up to the bluffs one mile beyond Malaga Cove after you round Flat Rock Point. The Shoreline Route continues along the Palos Verdes Estates Shoreline Preserve and rounds Rocky Point to Lunada Bay where a path leads up to the Bluff Route, 3.1 miles beyond Malaga Cove.

Leaving Point Vicente, hike the path on the west side of Palos Verdes Dr. South for 0.2 miles, and take the trail along the cliffs to Long Point and Terranea Resort. ....**total miles 13.3**

Looking North to Point Vicente

Day 3:
Long Point, Palos Verdes Peninsula to San Pedro Ferry Terminal and Santa Catalina

The shoreline along the northwest portion of Portuguese Bend (2.5 miles) may be impassable at high tide. Time your hike to reach this section between a few hours before and after low tide.

Leaving Terranea Resort, take the Vanderlip Link Trail along the bluffs to its end. Walk up Coastside Dr. Turn left on Beachview Dr., right on Seahill Dr, and right on Palos Verdes Dr. South to Abalone Cove Shoreline Park. ....**1.4 miles**

Continue along the shoulder of Palos Verdes Dr. South. You will see Pepper Tree Dr. intersecting Palos Verdes Dr. South on the left. 0.1

mile beyond Pepper Tree Dr., take the gravel road toward the sea. Pass through an archery range on the gravel road where you will find the trail to the shore at the southwest corner of the range ..**2.8 miles**

Follow the shore of Portuguese Bend to Half-way Point.......**3.9 miles**

Continue along the shoreline to Royal Palms County Beach, marked by tall palm trees and picnic tables. Take the paved road up to the bluffs and White Point. ....**6.2 miles.**

Stroll along the sidewalk and grassy bluffs of Point Fermin Park to Fermin Point ....**8.1 miles**

Leaving the park, take Shepard St., jog right and left on Bluff Pl., turn right on Stephen M. White Dr. and right on Oliver Vickery Circle. Walk through Cabrillo Beach Park and along Shoshonean Dr. Turn right on 22nd St. and left along the water front. Continue parallel to Harbor Blvd., to Vincent Thomas Bridge, and the San Pedro Ferry Terminal ....**total miles 12.3**

Enjoy a one hour ferry ride to beautiful Santa Catalina.

TRANSPORTATION

Flying into Los Angeles

Take a Super Shuttle van from Los Angeles International Airport to Santa Monica for $15 per person. For information and reservations call 800-258-3826 or try *www.supershuttle.com*. Super Shuttle also serves other L.A. area airports.

Ferry from San Pedro to Avalon, Santa Catalina

Ferries leave and return several times a day. It is wise to make reservations at *www.catalinaexpress.com* or 800-481-3470. Round trip tickets are $72.50.

Returning from San Pedro Ferry Terminal to Santa Monica

Visit *www.metro.net* for easy public transportation trip planning. The bus trip from San Pedro Catalina Terminal to Santa Monica should require one transfer, 60-90 minutes, and cost less than $3.

MAPS

The U.S. Geological Survey sells topographical hiking maps and provides free maps you can download. Visit *http://store.usgs.gov* and go to the map locator.

Day 1: Venice Quadrangle

Day 2: Redondo Beach Quadrangle

Day 3: San Pedro Quadrangle

Google Maps at *www.maps.google.com* is also a useful tool for viewing the shoreline and roadways adjacent to the shore.

PLACES TO STAY

LODGING COSTS

$ less than $100 | $$ $100-$150 | $$$ $150-$200 | $$$$ more than $200

Santa Monica

These inns are a short walk from Santa Monica Pier

Santa Monica Hostel
1436 2nd St.
310- 393-9913
http://www.hilosangeles.org
$
Great location
Singles from $30 per night
Continental breakfast
Private rooms available

Georgian Hotel
1415 Ocean Ave.
310- 395-9945
www.georgianhotel.com
$$$$

Doubletree Santa Monica
1707 4th St.
310- 395-3332
www.doubletree.com
$$$ - $$$$

Hotel Casa Del Mar
1910 Ocean Way
(310) 581-5533
http://www.hotelcasadelmar.com
$$$$

The Huntley Hotel
1111 2nd St.
310- 394-5454
http://www.thehuntleyhotel.com
$$$$

Ocean View Hotel
1447 Ocean Ave.
800-452-4888
www.oceanviewsantamonica.com
$$-$$$

Manhattan Beach

These inns are a short walk from the beach

Sea View Inn at the Beach
3400 Highland Ave.
310-545-1504
www.theseaviewinn.com
$$-$$$$

Turn inland 1.1 miles north of Manhattan Beach Pier
and walk 5 short blocks on 34th St. Fun neighborhood
with restaurants and bars. Complimentary bicycles,
beach chairs and towels, boogie boards.

Shade Hotel
1221 N Valley Dr.
310-546-4995
www.shadehotel.com
$$$$
5 blocks inland from pier

Long Point, Palos Verdes Peninsula

Terranea Resort
100 Terranea Way
866-802-8000
www.terranea.com
$$$$

San Pedro

Doubletree
2800 Via Cabrillo-Marina
310-514-3344
sanpedrodoubletree.com
$$-$$$$

Crowne Plaza Hotel
610 S. Palos Verdes St.
877-270-1393
www.crowneplaza.com
$$$-$$$$

Sunrise Hotel
525 Harbor Blvd.
310-548-1080
www.sunrisesanpedro.com
$-$$

HI-LA South Bay Hostel
3601 South Gaffey St.
Building 613
310-831-8109
www.hiusa.org/losangelessouthbay
$
In Angels Gate Park above Pt. Fermin

Santa Catalina, Avalon

A few of the many local inns
Zane Grey Pueblo Hotel
199 Chimes Rd.
800-378-3256
http://www.zanegreypueblohotel.com
$-$$$
Former home of western novelist

Aurora Hotel
137 Mirilla Ave.
310-510-0454
www.auroracatalina.com
$$-$$$

Inn on Mt. Ada
398 Wrigley Rd.
310-510-2030
www.innonmtada.com
$$$$
Former colonial mansion of chewing gum
magnate, Wm. Wrigley, Jr.

Old Turner Inn
232 Catalina Ave.
310-510-2236
www.oldturnerinn.com
$$-$$$

Hotel Mac Rae
409 Crescent Ave.
310-510-0246
www.hotelmacrae.com
$-$$$$

Hotel Catalina
129 Whittley Ave.
800-540-0184
www.hotelcatalina.com
$$-$$$$

Notes

3. Santa Catalina to Newport Beach

"The sea is emotion incarnate. It loves, hates, and weeps. It defies all attempts to capture it with words and rejects all shackles."

- Christopher Paolini, Eragon, 2002

*View of
Avalon Bay*

THIS EASY THREE DAY, 23.5 mile walkabout starts on the beautiful island of Santa Catalina. Enjoy the slow pace of island life. Explore Catalina's shoreline by kayak, and hike its rugged mountains. Then take the ferry to Long Beach and hike three days to Newport Beach, strolling on classic Southern California surfing and swimming beaches. Along the way, sample the delights of interesting seaside towns – good food, fun bars, live music, and unique inns.

> *"A good traveler has no fixed plans, and is not intent on arriving."*
>
> *- Lao-tzu, Tao Te Ching*

ITINERARY

DAY 1: Avalon, Santa Catalina to Seal Beach		**8.5**
DAY 2: Seal Beach to Huntington Beach		**9.2**
DAY 3: Huntington Beach to Newport Beach		**5.8**
TOTAL MILEAGE		**23.5**

Avalon, Santa Catalina

Start this three day walkabout in the town of Avalon and treat yourself to a few days on the island. Your ferry, the Catalina Express, docks in a deep blue harbor crowded with sailboats. Houses climb steep hillsides dense with eucalyptus, prickly pear cactus, and coastal chaparral. Restaurants, shops, hotels, and bars line the bayfront promenade.

Leaving the ferry, a gentle breeze refreshes. The air is sensual. You find yourself relaxing a few notches. Slow down, you are on island time.

This is a walking town with old world charm. Enjoy a stroll along the waterfront where colorful tiles decorate old buildings. Hike a mile to beautiful Wrigley Memorial and Botanical Garden, a serene sanctuary with cactus, trees, and plants unique to the Channel Islands. From there, hike Garden-to-Sky Trail, a four mile loop

Avalon

that climbs to 1,206 feet and a breathtaking viewpoint overlooking both sides of the island. Rent kayaks and explore the bay along a rugged coastline. Snorkel in the clear waters of Lovers Cove, and swim in kelp forests along with thousands of fish. If you have the time, obtain a permit from the Catalina Island Conservancy (*www.catalinaconservancy.org*, 310-510-2595), and spend a day hiking or biking the backcountry.

Santa Catalina, 22 miles long and 8 miles wide, is one of the

Avalon Sunset

Channel Islands. Despite the Four Preps' 1958 hit song, "26 Miles," it is only a mere 22 miles from the continent, but the boys captured the spirit. It is "the island of romance."

The island has been settled for 9,000 years. Here the Tongva people, whom the Spanish named Gabrielino, thrived. They were part of a powerful and wealthy people whose territory stretched from Topanga Canyon to Laguna Beach and throughout L.A. Basin. The island people mined and traded steatite (soapstone) with their mainland cousins and with other tribes, the Chumash to the north, the Luiseño to the south, and the Mojave to the east. The soft soapstone was prized for fashioning cooking pots, weights for digging sticks, pipes, charm stones, effigies, and ornaments.

The island Gabrielino first encountered Europeans in 1542 when Juan Rodriguez Cabrillo paid a brief visit on his expedition to explore the coast of New Spain and to find a new route to China. He stayed long enough to claim the island for the Spanish Crown and to name it San Salvador after his ship.

It was not until sixty years later, in 1602, that the next Europeans came calling. Three ships, led by Sebastian Vizcáino, arrived on the eve of Saint Catherine's day, November 24. He renamed the island to honor the saint.

The expedition's mission was to explore and map the California Coast. Carmelite Father, Antonio de la Ascencion, described meeting the island Gabrielino in his journal.

On the 27th of the month they dropped anchor in a very good cove where a multitude of Indians came out in canoes of cedar and pine, made of planks very well joined and caulked each one with eight oars and with fourteen or fifteen Indians, who looked like galley slaves. They came alongside without the slightest fear and came on board our ships, mooring their own. They showed great pleasure at seeing us...

The men of the expedition suffered from hunger and scurvy, and the Gabrielino greeted them with gifts of sardines and a sweet potato-like tuber. The Gabrielino were great seafarers who lived from the bounty of the ocean. Ascencion described their technique.

The manner of fishing among the Indians is very ingenious, easy, & pleasant. They carry in their boats long and thin poles, and to one of these fix a harpoon made of fish bones, fastening to the harpoon a long rope. When they perceive at the bot-

tom near the rocks a sea wolf (sea lion) or any other fish worth
catching, they strike it with the harpoon; then vere out the rope,
till the fish being spent, they draw it ashore if large; and if small
into the boat. Thus they catch as many fish as they please. The
sea wolves serve them both for food and cloathing.

The Spanish invasion of missionaries and soldiers later brought
disease and subjugation. Archaeological analysis of midden sites
suggests that in 2000 BCE, as many as 2,500 Gabrielino lived on
the island. By the 1830s the Catalina Island Gabrielino were gone.
They had perished or migrated to the mainland to work in missions
or as ranch hands.

My wife, Heidi, and I along with our friends, Lesley and Barry,
took this walkabout in late September, a great season for a long
hike on the Southern California Coast. While it was scorching
inland, with temperatures over 100 degrees, air and water temperatures along the coast were in the 70s. Evenings were balmy and
sublime. School was in session, so the beaches were uncrowded.

Avalon has dozens of charming inns. We stayed in the older,
funky Zane Grey Pueblo Hotel, a former home of the famed early
twentieth century author of 54 novels set in the American West. It
sits high on a hill, surrounded by steep chaparral covered slopes,
overlooking Avalon Bay. Mule deer wander off the hills and
through the patio around the swimming pool.

You will probably find it difficult to leave Avalon, but it is time
to take a hike from inn to inn.

Day 1: Avalon, Santa Catalina to Seal Beach

The 22 mile ferry ride from Santa Catalina to the Long Beach Ferry
Terminal takes an hour. Freighters and tankers patiently rest in San
Pedro Bay, waiting their turn to enter L.A. or Long Beach Harbor.
The ferry sails into the harbor passing wide berths where longshore-

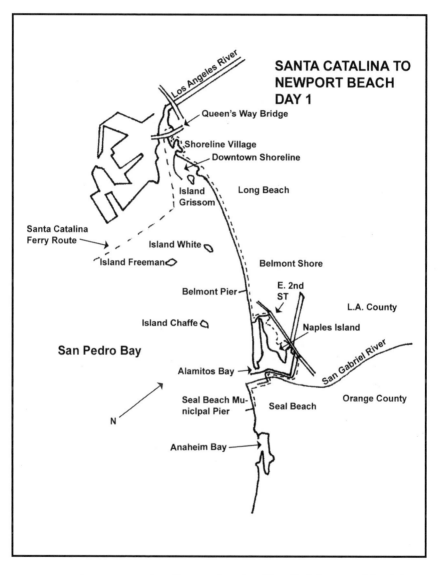

men steer giant cranes loading and unloading freighters with eigh-teen wheeler sized containers. The retired ocean liner, RMS Queen Mary, is permanently berthed here. From 1936 to 1967 she sailed between England and New York, a leisurely and luxurious way to travel. During World War II, she ferried soldiers and supplies across the Atlantic, outrunning enemy ships. Now, she is a Long Beach tourist attraction with restaurants, a hotel, and museum.

Leaving the ferry, turn right and hike the waterfront keeping the water on your right. Please see The Route for directions. Pass through Shoreline Village, where you can stop for breakfast, and

Alamitos Bay

stroll along the vast Downtown Shoreline Marina to the beach.

Walk the shore or the winding walking path. The densely urban city of Long Beach is mostly obscured by high bluffs. The bay is protected by a long breakwater that starts near Point Fermin in San Pedro and extends 8.5 miles, sheltering the ports of Los Angeles and Long Beach. Together they are the fifth busiest port in the world.

Waves are mild along the crescent shore of Long Beach, protected by the breakwater and islands, both natural and artificial, that dot San Pedro Bay. The small artificial islands are built for oil wells. Tropical landscaping and fake high rises mask and hide the oil rigs. The beach can be crowded during the summer and on weekends, but was less populated on the late September weekday when we hiked.

Pass Belmont Pier, a popular fishing spot, and follow The Route for the turn inland around Alamitos Bay. We stopped along the narrow peninsula beyond the turn for a swim in the Pacific. The waters were luxurious, warm enough to linger for hours.

Lesley's father had been in the oil business. She grew up all over the world, but her family lived in Belmont Shore when they were in the States. This was a trip down memory lane for her, and she served as our guide as we hiked through her childhood haunts. After a swim in the ocean, we crossed the two block wide spit and swam in the calm waters of Alamitos Bay before strolling to East Second St. and the Open Sesame restaurant for a Mediterranean lunch of baba ghanoush, stuffed grape leaves, fattoush, shawarma, and kabobs at a sidewalk table.

Take a brief detour off busy East Second St. and enter the tranquil residential neighborhood of Naples Island. Walk to Riyo Alto Canal. Descend the steps and stroll the sidewalk bordering the canal past lovely houses with lush rose gardens and stately palms. Stand up paddle boarders ply the quiet waters and pleasure craft line the wide, arcing channel, berthed at private docks.

Return to East Second St., cross a bridge over Alamitos Bay and another over San Gabriel River, the demarcation of the border of L.A. and Orange Counties. The river winds 60 miles through Los Angeles Basin from its source in the San Gabriel Mountains. This was the heart of Tongva-Gabielinos territory.

Their third encounter with Europeans came 167 years after Vizcáino, this time a land expedition in 1769 led by Don Gaspar de Portolá. This time the results would be fatal.

Portolá traveled from Mexico leading a "sacred expedition" of 62 soldiers, priests, and Indian servants along with 200 horses and mules. They met Father Junipero Serra in San Diego. Their joint task was to explore and secure Spain's claim on *Nueva California* by establishing missions and settlements. Serra stayed in San Diego to found the first mission while Portolá headed north to search for Monterey Bay, the "protected harbor" discovered and praised by Vizcáino. He overshot Monterey, but his party stumbled upon San Francisco Bay becoming the first Europeans to view what Father Juan Crespi called, "this most noble estuary."

Soon after leaving San Diego, they entered the land of the Tong-va-Gabrielino. What a strange and frightening sight they must have been - priests in long cloth robes, and soldiers dressed in six-ply deerskin vests, riding horses and each armed with a lance, sword, and musket. The Gabrielino greeted the newcomers with dried fish, acorn pinole, chia seeds, and other delicacies. Ensign Miguel Costansó wrote of the encounter in his journal.

> *We pitched our camp on the left bank of the river. To the right there is a populous Indian village; the inhabitants received us with great kindness. Fifty-two of them came to our quarters and their captain asked us by signs which we understood easily, to remain there and live with them. (He said) that they would provide antelopes, hares, or seeds for our subsistence, that the lands which we saw were theirs, and they would share them with us.*

The village had conical shaped, tule thatched houses 15 to 30 feet in diameter, housing a family or as many as 30 people. Women grew their hair long and wore skirts woven of tule or grass. Men wore only a belt to carry food or tools and capes made of deer or sea otter skins. They wore their hair loose or braided, held in place by a bone hairpin, and both sexes painted their bodies and faces black and red in patterns to indicate social status, one's home village, or for decoration.

Canals – Naples Island

Portolá moved on, but on September 8, 1771, the Franciscans founded *Mission San Gabriel Arcángel* in Gabrielino territory. It was the fourth of what was to be 21 missions. Originally built on Rio Hondo, a tributary of San Gabriel River, it was relocated after flooding in 1776 to its current site, the village of *Iisanchanga*, present day San Gabriel. From the mission, the Tongva people were given their Spanish name.

The mission system intended to baptize California Indians, teach them a trade, and then free them to be productive Christians. They were to live and work on the mission lands as neophytes for a decade, then be given their own land. Instead, they were lured by clothes, food, and blankets, then imprisoned and made to work the mission land to support the priests and soldiers. They were punished with the stock and the lash. If they escaped, soldiers hunted them down.

Toypuina was a girl of nine years at the time of the Spanish invasion. She grew to be a shaman, trader, and orator. She despised the Spanish for taking her people's land, for the diseases they brought that were killing her people, and for their brutality.

In 1785, at the age of 24, she organized men of seven villages to attack the mission, intending to kill the padres and soldiers. They scaled the mission walls armed with bows and arrows, but word of the attack had leaked out and the Spanish were ready. With a shout of "Santiago," the patron saint of Spain, the soldiers attacked first. The Indians fled. Toypuina and 20 others were captured and thrown into the mission jail.

Legend tells us that at her trial, she entered the courtroom with her hands tied behind her back. Told to sit, she kicked over the stool, stood erect and fierce, telling the judge, "I hate the padres and all of you, for living here on my native soil, for trespassing upon the land of my forefathers and despoiling our tribal domains."

She was sentenced to a forced conversion and banishment to *San Carlos Borroméo de Carmelo Mission* in the north. She never returned to the land she loved.

The San Gabriel River has been altered since Toypuina's time. It once meandered through the grasslands of L.A. Basin. Periodic floods would send it careening over its banks to find a new course.

Today it is restrained by dams and flood control channels.

After crossing the river, follow the bike path to the shore and walk a short distance to Seal Beach Pier. Seal Beach has a history of being a working class, Navy town. After walking by urban Long

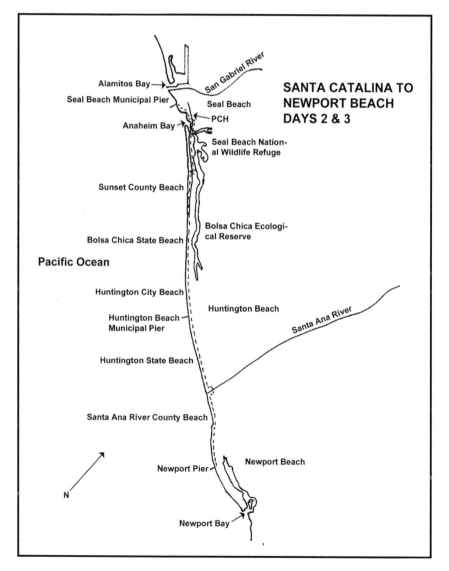

SANTA CATALINA TO NEWPORT BEACH DAYS 2 & 3

Alamitos Bay

San Gabriel River

Seal Beach Municipal Pier

Seal Beach

PCH

Anaheim Bay

Seal Beach National Wildlife Refuge

Sunset County Beach

Bolsa Chica Ecological Reserve

Bolsa Chica State Beach

Pacific Ocean

Huntington City Beach

Huntington Beach

Huntington Beach Municipal Pier

Santa Ana River

Huntington State Beach

Santa Ana River County Beach

Newport Beach

Newport Pier

N

Newport Bay

Beach and through the upscale neighborhoods of Belmont Shore and Naples, it feels like a throwback to a bygone era. This is a little known treasure of the Southern California Coast with a beautiful wide beach. Main Street extends three blocks inland from the pier. It is lined with tourist stores, ice cream shops, restaurants, and bars, more than enough to keep an inn-to-inn hiker entertained for an evening.

Day 2: Seal Beach to Huntington Beach

Leaving Seal Beach Pier, hike the shoreline or paved walkway. The Seal Beach Naval Weapons Station blocks further beach access at 0.5 miles, so follow The Route around the station, crossing a bridge over Anaheim Bay. This is one of the longest stretches of hiking along the Pacific Coast Highway on the entire 200 mile Southern California Coast walkabout, 1.6 miles, but a wide bike lane and a sand path provide ample distance from traffic to keep this section interesting and enjoyable. Egrets and herons wade in the tidal marshlands of the Seal Beach National Wildlife Refuge on the east side of the PCH.

Turn right on Anderson St. and return to the shore at Sunset Beach or walk the wide, grassy promenade just one short block inland from the beach. Bolsa Chica State Beach begins where the houses of Sunset Beach end. The beach is broad and inviting, but the tide was high when we hiked, the sand soft and slow, so we strolled the paved walkway at the top of the beach. Scores of surfers caught three foot waves just offshore.

From the walkway you can look across the PCH to Bolsa Chica Ecological Reserve. Shallow waters wind through tidal marshes. The reserve, along with Seal Beach National Wildlife Refuge provides crucial habitat and a winter sanctuary for migrating birds on the Pacific Flyway. They are a home for the endangered California

Blufftop Park

least tern and the light-footed clapper rail.

We passed a fenced off area of dune protecting hundreds of tiny snowy plover, grey and white birds that crowded the sand between scruffy, low foliage. Nestling into small depressions, they made a noisy clamor of chatter, trills, and whistles. The western snowy plover is a threatened species under the Endangered Species Act. Breeding in rookeries of sparsely vegetated sand beaches and dunes makes them vulnerable to humans and dogs. The fences give them a fighting chance.

After returning to the beach, we saw small flocks of plovers feeding in the surf. They sprinted after a receding wave on tiny legs, furiously pecking the sand for insects and crustaceans. The next wave crashed, and they flew away in unison showing a flash of black and white on their under wings. Coasting down the beach, the search was repeated. It seemed they surely must be burning more calories than they were consuming.

Cross a bridge at the outlet of Bolsa Chica estuary and return to the beach, or hike the paved walkway along Blufftop Park to Huntington Pier.

Huntington Beach is celebrated in song and lore as Surf City. I had vivid dreams of this spot as a teenager growing up in the Midwest. It has lost most of the charm it possessed in the 60s when Jan and Dean sang it praises, and I doubt there are still "two girls for every boy," but it remains a very popular surfing beach.

Huntington State Beach

There are several inns within a few blocks of the pier. The Huntington Surf Inn is a friendly and funky establishment just three blocks north of the pier. It has been a favorite spot of surfers for years. Rooms are eclectically designed with walls covered in weathered driftwood or painted bright, ocean blue with crashing waves. Ask for Room 9 for the best views and a nice cross breeze.

Most of the action in Huntington Beach - shops, bars, and restaurants – is on or near Main St. It was crowded and festive with well-oiled celebrants on the balmy weekday evening of our visit.

Day 3: Huntington Beach to Newport Beach

Get ready to enjoy a 5.8 mile stroll along perhaps the ultimate
Southern California beach – spacious, flat firm footing, inviting
waves, and great people watching. You may want to hike this one
in your bathing suit, maybe even barefoot, so you can jump in the
Pacific when you get the urge.

Try the Sugar Shack on Huntington's Main St. for a friendly and
hearty breakfast at a sidewalk table in the morning sunshine.

Hike southeast on the shore or along the paved walkway on
Huntington City Beach for a mile and Huntington State Beach
for another 2.5. The state beach has a protected preserve for the
California least tern, who summer on Southern California beaches
from April to August and then head south to Mexico and Central
America for the winter. They numbered in the thousands before
their wetland habitat was gobbled by development and their beach
nesting grounds became crowded. By 1974 the flocks had dwindled
to 582 mating pairs, but conservation measures helped increase
their numbers to 6,500 pairs in 2004. We passed a sign at the edge
of the preserve, hand written in June, recording 534 nests, 205 eggs,
and 163 chicks.

We were fortunate. A few remained in late September. A half
dozen of the small gulls, very white with black masks, orange
beaks, and a forked tail, still grazed along the shore.

At 3.5 miles, take a jog around the mouth of Santa Ana River,
the largest river in Southern California. Starting high in the San
Bernardino Mountains, it winds for 96 miles and drains a water-
shed of 2,650 square miles.

Gaspar de Portolá's party crossed the river and camped in a valley at the base of a mountain range on July 26, 1769 the feast day

of Saint Anne. They named the valley in her honor. While camping on the banks of the river, a powerful earthquake struck. They
christened it El Rio del Dulcissimo de Jesus de los Temblores. It
was soon renamed Rio de Santa Anna.

Santa Ana River County Beach begins south of the river. The
paved walkway ends. Hike the shore or take an easy stroll on residential streets paralleling the beach until 36th St. where the paved
Ocean Walk begins.

Hike to Newport Pier. Newport Beach has retained its allure
as a fun beach town. The neighborhood at the base of the pier is
crowded with restaurants and bars. Fans throng into multi-screen
sports bars. Live music pours out of taverns and onto the streets
on warm evenings any night of the week. Try Rockin' Baja Lobster

Tern Count

Belmont Shore Pier

for a Mexican lunch or dine on steaks and sea food with live blues, jazz, or rock at Blue Beet. Stay the night at one of Newport's many inns, and celebrate the conclusion of a beautiful 23.5 mile hike from inn to inn on the Southern California Coast.

THE ROUTE

The entire route of this three day walkabout should be passable, even at high tide, but walking the beach may be slow during the hours before and after high tide. Hiking the paved walkways at the top of beaches or walking neighborhood streets are pleasant alternatives to hiking a soft shoreline. Expect to find the best beach hiking – flat and firm sand – in the hours before and after low tide. Tide schedules are available at *http://tidesandcurrents.noaa.gov/ tide_predictions.shtm.*

All mileages listed for a given day are cumulative.

Avalon, Santa Catalina to Long Beach Ferry Terminal

The Catalina Express ferry terminal (www.catalinaexpress.com, 800-481-3470) is at the base of Queensway Bridge in downtown Long Beach.

Day 1: Avalon, Santa Catalina to Seal Beach

After departing the ferry from Santa Catalina, turn right heading southeast along the water's edge. Keep the water on your right as you wind under the Queensway Bridge, past Aquarium of the Pacific, through Shoreline Village, along the vast downtown Shoreline Marina, to the beach. Walk the shore of San Pedro Bay or the winding paved walkway at the top of the beach to Belmont Pier.................**3.4 miles**

Nesting Snowy Plover

RMS Queen Mary

Continue along the Belmont Shore beach. Turn inland when you see a solitary blue house at the top of the beach. This is also the end of the paved walkway. Walk up 54th Place or along the shore of Alamitos Bay to East Second St. ....**4.8 miles**

Turn right on busy East Second St., quickly cross a bridge, and turn right on The Toledo through the quiet neighborhoods of Naples Island. Walk five short blocks, and descend the stairs to Canal Rivo Alto. Take the sidewalk along the canal. Ascend the steps at the second bridge, and continue along The Toledo. Turn left on East Naples Plaza back to East Second St. and turn right. Cross the bridge and angle right on North Marina Dr. Cross the bridge over San Gabriel River, and turn right on First St. Turn left on Ocean Ave. or walk the bike path along the river to the beach. Turn left to Seal Beach Pier. ....
....**total miles 8.5**

Catalina Deer

Day 2: Seal Beach to Huntington Beach

Hike south from Seal Beach Pier along the shoreline or the paved walkway to the end of the beach. Turn left on Seal Beach Blvd. and right on Pacific Coast Highway. Hike the path adjacent to a wide bike lane, cross a bridge over Anaheim Bay, and turn right on Anderson St. to Sunset Beach. ....**2.6 miles**

Hike the shoreline or walk one block inland along the grassy promenade that runs the length of Sunset Beach to where houses along the top of the beach end at Bolsa Chica State Beach. ....**3.8 miles**

Continue along Bolsa Chica State Beach on the shoreline or paved walkway to Huntington Beach Pier. .... **total miles 9.2**

Day 3: Huntington Beach to Newport Beach

Hike southeast along the shore of Huntington City Beach and Huntington State Beach or the paved walkway at the top of the beach to Santa Ana River. ....**3.4 miles**

Leave the beach to cross the river and return to Santa Ana River County Beach. The paved walkway ends. You can walk through the neighborhoods one block off the beach, returning to the paved walkway along the top of the beach at 36th St. or hike the shoreline to Newport Pier. ....**total miles 5.8**

TRANSPORTATION

Flying into Los Angeles

Take a Super Shuttle van from Los Angeles International Airport to Long Beach Catalina Ferry Terminal. The cost is $30 for the first person and $9 for a second. For information and reservations call 800-258-3826 or try *www.supershuttle.com*. Super Shuttle also serves other L.A. area airports.

Ferry from Long Beach to Avalon, Santa Catalina and return

Ferries leave and return several times a day. It is wise to make reservations at *www.catalinaexpress.com* or 800-481-3470. Round trip tickets are $72.50.

Returning from Newport Beach to Long Beach

Visit *www.metro.net* for easy public transportation trip planning. The bus trip from Newport Beach to Long Beach Catalina Ferry Terminal should take 60-90 minutes and cost less than $2.

MAPS

The U.S. Geological Survey sells topographical hiking maps and provides free maps you can download. Visit *http://store.usgs.gov* and go to the map locator.

Day 1: Long Beach Quadrangle

Day 1 and 2: Seal Beach Quadrangle

Day 3: Newport Beach OE S Quadrangle

Google Maps at *www.maps.google.com* is also a useful tool for viewing the shoreline and roadways adjacent to the shore.

PLACES TO STAY

LODGING COSTS

$ less than $100 | $$ $100-$150 | $$$ $150-$200 | $$$$ more than $200

Santa Catalina, Avalon

A few of many local inns

Zane Grey Pueblo Hotel
199 Chimes Rd.
310-510-0966
www.zanegreypueblohotel.com
$-$$$
Former home of western novelist

Aurora Hotel
137 Mirilla Ave.
310-510-0454
www.auroracatalina.com
$$-$$$

Inn on Mt. Ada
398 Wrigley Rd.
310-510-2030

www.innonmtada.com
$$$$
Former colonial mansion of chewing gum
magnate, Wm. Wrigley, Jr.

Old Turner Inn
232 Catalina Ave.
310-510-2236
www.oldturnerinn.com
$$-$$$

Hotel Mac Rae
409 Crescent Ave.
310-510-0246
www.hotelmacrae.com
$-$$$$

Hotel Catalina
129 Whittley Ave.
800-540-0184
www.hotelcatalina.com
$$-$$$$

Seal Beach

The Pacific Inn
600 Marina Dr.
866-466-0300
www.thepacificinn.com
$$-$$$
Four blocks from beach and pier

Hampton Inn and Suites
2401 Seal Beach Blvd.
562-594-3939
www.hamptoninn.hilton.com
$$-$$$
0.75 miles from beach

1.3 miles from pier

Huntington Beach

Inns near Huntington Beach Pier

Huntington Surf Inn
720 Pacific coast Hwy.
714-536-2444
www.huntingtonsurfinn.com
$$-$$$

Shorebreak Hotel
500 Pacific Coast Hwy.
714-861-4470
www.shorebreakhotel.com
$$$$

Sun'n Sands Motel
1102 Pacific Coast Hwy.
714-536-2543
www.sunnsands.com
$$-$$$

Hilton Waterfront Beach Resort
21100 Pacific Coast Hwy.
714-845-8000
www.hilton.com
$$$-$$$$

Hyatt Regency Resort and Spa
21500 Pacific Coast Hwy.
714-698-1234
www.huntingtonbeach.hyatt.com
$$$$

Newport Beach

Inns near Newport Pier

Bay Shores Peninsula Hotel
1800 W. Balboa Blvd.
800-222-6675
www.thebestinn.com
$$-$$$$

Doryman's Newport Beach Hotel and Inn
2102 W. Oceanfront
949-675-7300
www.dorymansinn.com
$$$$

Newport Beachwalk Hotel
2306 W. Oceanfront Blvd.
800-571-8749
www.newportbeachwalkhotel.com
$$$$

Little Inn by the Bay
29277 Newport Blvd.
800-438-4466
www.littleinnbythebay.com

$$-$$$$

Notes

Notes

4. Newport Beach to San Clemente

*"I like this place and willingly could
waste my time in it."*

- William Shakespeare, As You Like It

*View
Approaching Laguna Beach*

THIS MODERATE FOUR DAY, 27.3 mile walkabout hikes some of the most alluring swimming and surfing beaches in the world as well as rugged rocky shores under steep cliffs that you will share with sea birds, seals, and dolphins. You'll visit lively classic beach towns, step back in time in the beautifully restored cabins of Crystal Cove, and savor the fine cuisine and arts scene of Laguna Beach. Explore the Southern California Riviera at two miles an hour, hiking inn-to-inn.

"Adopt the pace of nature: her secret is patience."

- Ralph Waldo Emerson, Nature

ITINERARY

DAY 1:	Newport Beach to Crystal Cove State Park	**7.2**
DAY 2:	Crystal Cove State Park to Laguna Beach	**4.6**
DAY 3:	Laguna Beach to Dana Point	**9.5**
DAY 4:	Dana Point to San Clemente Pier	**6.0**
TOTAL MILEAGE		**27.3**

Day 1: Newport Beach to Crystal Cove State Park

Newport Beach has the feel of an old-time Southern California beach town. You may want to kick off this 27 mile adventure by enjoying some of the many eateries and watering holes surrounding the Newport Pier. My wife, Heidi, and I hiked this walkabout in early spring, during March Madness. Morning haze burned off bringing warm, sunny afternoons. The evenings were balmy. Newport's multi-screened sports bars were packed with exuberant college basketball fans. Live music spilled out of taverns and onto the streets.

In the morning, visit the funky Dory Fleet Market at the base of the pier. Local fishers set out to sea in small boats as early as 2:00am, returning to sell their catch to restaurants and directly to the public. The market has been operating since 1891, and it feels

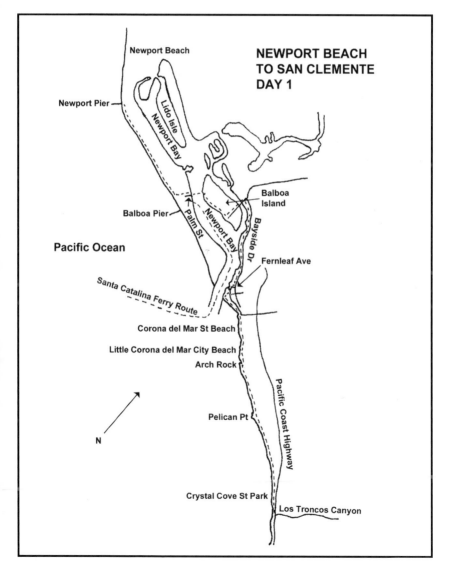

like you are stepping back in time. Seagulls circle, scavenging for scraps, while customers line up early to buy rock cod, snapper, butter fish, stone crab, abalone, lobster, or shrimp. There is a festive mood as fishers and their families fillet, weigh, and wrap your catch-of-the-day.

Newport Ocean Walk

There are a handful of inns close to the pier. The Bay Shores Peninsula Hotel is relatively modest in price with a helpful staff, fresh baked cookies, and spacious rooms with painted surfing murals. One short block from the beach, they will provide you with beach towels, chairs, and boogie boards.

Our hike starts by walking the Newport Peninsula along the shoreline or the paved Ocean Front Promenade. The broad beach

Balboa Island Ferry Stop

is crowded on summer afternoons with sunbaked beach lovers, but on this early spring morning, we shared the beach only with a flock of tiny sanderlings passing through on their way to Artic breeding grounds. They grazed along the ocean's edge, racing out to probe the sand as a wave receded, then dashing inland before the next surge.

Take the Balboa Island Ferry for a short ride from Newport Peninsula, across Newport Bay, to Balboa Island. It only costs $1, and the crossing takes a few minutes. The man-made island was created by developers in the early 1900s by dredging the estuary, also forming the bay, which now is the home berth for over 9,000 boats. Houses fill small island lots with some of the most densely crowded and expensive real estate in the country. On this spring

Rocky Shoreline South of Corona del Mar

morning, beautiful houses had flower boxes overflowing with roses, Iceland poppies, bright geraniums, and lush bearded iris.

Hike through the island, crossing Marine Ave. Bridge to the mainland. (Please see The Route for detailed directions.) Pass by ice cream stores, bars, restaurants, and shops selling beach wear and overpriced tourist trinkets.

After a walk along the harbor and through the neighborhood, you reach Corona del Mar State Beach. You can choose to stay on pavement to Crystal Cove State Park or hike the shoreline. There are rocky stretches along the shore, but they are easily passable at lower tides. Tide schedules are available at ***http://tidesandcurrents. noaa.gov/tide_predictions.shtm***. The coast route is beautiful, and it was a joy to hike an hour or two after low tide. There are frequent public stairways. If it is difficult to pass spots along the rocky shoreline, take the stairs and walk residential streets until you can return to the beach.

After a stroll along Corona del Mar State Beach, the coastline changes to boulders and rock shelves. It is slow going, very rugged and beautiful. You will probably have the shoreline to yourself. Rock monoliths stand just offshore, resting spots for pelicans and cormorants. Stop to inspect the tide pools, home to sea snails, anemone, and hermit crabs. Harbor seals swim and feed beyond the breakers.

We stopped at Little Corona del Mar City Beach. Marbled godwits and willets on stilt-like legs probed the sand with long beaks. A pair of migrating mallards glided down a gully and joined them to graze at the water's edge.

Arch Rock

Return to a rocky stretch for another 0.5 mile and pass Arch Rock, a weathered offshore outcropping pierced by a window eroded from centuries of pounding waves. Massive boulders of sedimentary rock, uplifted from the ancient seabed, stand twisted and bent in the surf.

Crystal Cove State Beach extends for the next 3.5 miles, sandy but strewn with rocks. Fifty foot bluffs of sand and shale line the beach. Rocky reefs running perpendicular to the shore stretch into the surf. The footing is firm, and you can stride out.

Hike the beach to the historic district where ramshackle cottages from the 1930s – 1950s perch on the bluffs. The state park along with Crystal Cove Alliance is in the process of rescuing them. Thirteen individual and three dorm-style cottages have been meticu-

Crystal Cove Cabin

Twisted Rock Crystal Cove

lously restored along the beach, on the bluffs and up Los Trancos
Canyon. They are available for rent, but make your reservation
early. (See Places to Stay.) They may be booked months in advance.
The Beachcomber Cafe has a bar and serves a full menu for break-
fast, lunch and dinner (reservation line: 949-376-6900). Ruby's
Shake Shack serves burgers and shakes.

You may want to combine the first two legs of this walkabout
into a 12 mile day, but this is a very special place. As evening approaches, only cottage guests remain, and secluded Crystal Cove
State Park is a magical setting to spend the night. If you do combine the first two legs, and continue on to Laguna Beach, Crystal
Cove is a good place for a rest and lunch.

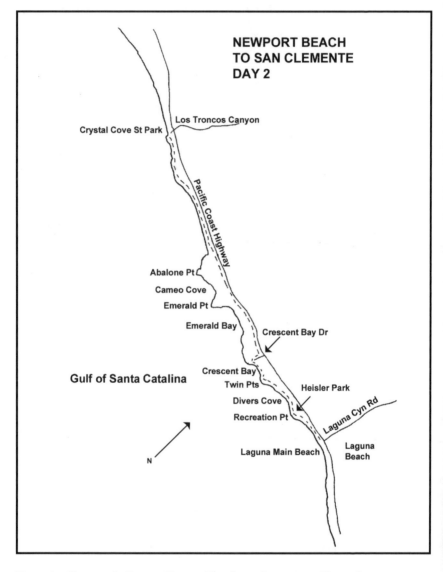

NEWPORT BEACH
TO SAN CLEMENTE
DAY 2

Los Troncos Canyon

Crystal Cove St Park

Pacific Coast Highway

Abalone Pt

Cameo Cove

Emerald Pt

Emerald Bay

Crescent Bay Dr

Gulf of Santa Catalina

Crescent Bay

Twin Pts

Divers Cove

Recreation Pt

Heisler Park

Laguna Cyn Rd

N

Laguna Main Beach

Laguna
Beach

Day 2: Crystal Cove State Park to Laguna Beach

Continue down the beach of Crystal Cove State Park rounding Reef
Point. Sixty foot cliffs border the broad, flat beach, and the footing
is firm. At 1.7 miles, the coast is blocked by rocky cliffs. Our trail

Crystal Cove State Beach

leaves the shoreline for a 1.3 mile walk along the wide bike lane of Pacific Coast Highway. Return to the shore at Crescent Bay.

There are two beautiful routes for the final 1.4 miles to the main beach of Laguna Beach. If the tide is low, hike around rocky Twin Points and Recreation Point, which separate the sandy beaches of Santa Ana Cove, Fishermans Cove, and Divers Cove. Enjoy the tide pools along the way. You can also hike along the bluffs from Crescent Bay to the main beach with a stroll through Heisler Park. In the spring, the park's beautiful coastal gardens are blooming with red and yellow roses, birds of paradise, and pride of Madeira sporting long spikes dense with deep blue blossoms. The walk along the bluffs offers striking views of the coves and the endless Pacific.

Both the shoreline and Heisler Park routes bring you to Laguna Beach's main beach. It is almost always a scene of strollers on the promenade, musicians, painters, beach volleyball, Frisbee, and sun bathers. This is a fun town, worth staying an extra day – lots of inns close to the beach and over seventy restaurants. There is a thriving arts community with more than 100 galleries and artists' studios. Enjoy live music on the street or in the bars.

Mid-summer features the popular Pageant of the Masters. Costumed actors recreate classic and contemporary paintings while an orchestra performs original pieces. Traffic, parking? No problem for an inn-to-inn hiker.

Day 3: Laguna Beach to Dana Point

Hike south on broad, flat Laguna Beach. Crowds thin as you leave the main beach behind. In the early morning, we saw some of the best surfing of the entire 200 mile Southern California Coast Walkabout. Dozens of surfers caught 3-4 foot waves along the surf break, but farther out to sea, large sets of waves surged over a rock shelf. A handful of masters caught 10-15 foot giants. They paddled out to meet a steep face, then turned and sprinted. Their boards caught the wave's energy and started to glide. A one motion hop from prone to

North from Dana Point Preserve

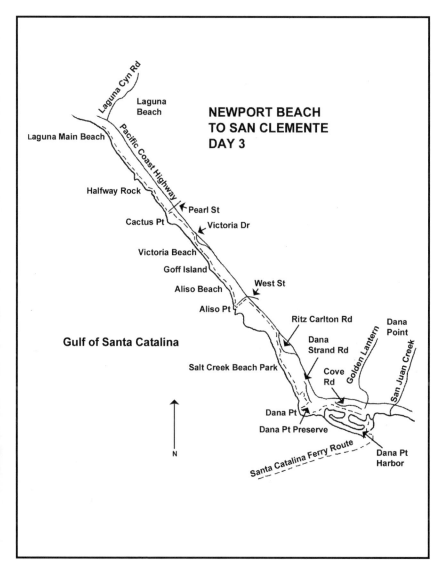

upright, and they were speeding across a crescent wall of water leaning left and right, making abrupt turns, dragging a hand in the water out of sheer joy. Then turning into the wave, they climbed over the crest, flopped into the sea, and paddled out for another ride.

After 1.3 miles, you reach Cactus Point, a rocky promontory that blocks the beach. Peer through a natural window and see the rugged coast line beyond. It is impassable. A short walk up the stairs and through the neighborhood offers a chance to see how folks are living on the edge of the Pacific. Public stairs lined with beautiful gardens descend to hidden coves.

Return to the shore and hike wide, sandy Victoria Beach to Goff Island. Round the peninsula to reach Aliso Beach. The way may be blocked if the tide is in, but stairs lead up to a walkway along the cliffs and through lush gardens of aloes, cactus, and flowering pride of Madeira. Another stairway returns to Aliso Beach. A snack bar near the parking lot serves breakfast or lunches of burgers, hot dogs, and salads. We stopped to rest and watch families enjoying the picnic area and playground. A pod of dolphins swam north just beyond the breakers, their black dorsal fins rising from the sea with each breath.

The shoreline route is blocked at the end of Aliso Beach. Climb the stairs and walk the sidewalk and wide bike lane along Pacific Coast Highway past gated communities. This is the longest stretch of hiking on the PCH (2.2 miles) for the entire 200 mile walkabout from Leo Carrillo State Beach to Mexico.

Turn toward the shore at Ritz Carlton Drive. You can stop at the Ritz-Carlton for the night, rather than continuing to Dana Point, and enjoy the hotel's luxurious accommodations and beautiful grounds overlooking the Pacific. This would shorten Day 3 by three miles and add them to Day 4.

Otherwise, descend through Bluff Park to Salt Creek Beach where there is a burger-burrito stand. The rocky bluffs of Dana Point block the route at the end of the broad beach, but after a climb up stairs, you enter the magical world of Dana Point Preserve.

A path winds along coastal cliffs through a wild garden of coyote brush, prickly pear cactus, cholla, fragrant coastal sagebrush, flat topped buckwheat, yellow bush sunflower, dove weed, and California buckeye. Lush native foliage attracts a wide variety of bird life. We felt as if we were transported back in time to the days before California's great cities were built and her shoreline crowded with houses.

Cactus Point

Leaving the preserve, the trail follows the cliffs overlooking Dana Point Harbor, a man-made structure, very different from the original shoreline.

Richard Henry Dana, Jr. visited this section of California Coast as a sailor aboard the Brig Pilgrim in 1834. He wrote about the journey in his masterpiece, "Two Years Before the Mast." His ship

Brig Pilgrim

left Boston, rounded Cape Horn, and sailed to Mexican California. There were Catholic Missions and a few small towns. "...we were in the remote parts of the earth, on an almost desert coast, in a country where there is neither law nor gospel..." But, there were large cattle ranches, and the Pilgrim came to trade for hides, "California banknotes."

Californians were hungry for luxury goods, and the Brig Pilgrim anchored below these cliffs to trade with the people of San Juan Capistrano. Dana fell in love with this section of coast.

"San Juan is the only romantic spot on the coast. The country here for several miles is high tableland, running boldly to the

shore, and breaking off in a steep cliff, at the foot of which the waters of the Pacific are constantly dashing. For several miles the water washes the very base of the hill, or breaks upon ledges and fragments of rocks which run out into the sea. Just where we landed was a small cove, or bight, which gave us, at high tide, a few square feet of sand beach between the sea and the bottom of the hill. This was the only landing place. Directly before us rose the perpendicular height of four or five hundred feet."

They climbed the cliffs.

"Here the country stretched out for miles, as far as the eye could reach, on a level, table surface, and the only habitation in sight was the small white mission of San Juan Capistrano, with a few Indian huts about it, standing in a small hallow..."

The cliffs were too steep to porter the hides down, so...

"Down the height we pitched the hides, throwing them as far out into the air as we could; and as they were all large, stiff, and doubled, like the cover of a book, the wind took them, and they swayed and eddied about, plunging and rising in the air, like a kite when it has broken its string. As it was now low tide, there was no danger of their falling into the water; and, as fast as they came to ground, the men below picked them up, and taking them on their heads, walked off with them to the boat."

Today, that scene is replaced by a tranquil swimming beach and harbor. Stop to pay a visit to a replica of the Brig Pilgrim berthed in the harbor and operated by Ocean Institute. After reading Dana's account of months at sea, the treacherous journey around Cape Horn, and stories of his fellow sailors and officers, I was shocked by how small the Brig Pilgrim was.

Stand up paddle boarders cruise the calm waters of Dana Point Harbor. Children splash along the beach, and picnickers play on the lawns of Heritage Park. Commercial fishing boats and pleasure craft from two person skiffs to luxury yachts crowd the marina. There are restaurants along the water's edge and lodging nearby, with many more inns along Pacific Coast Highway, a short distance from the harbor.

Day 4: Dana Point to San Clemente

The final day of this walkabout is a 6.0 mile stroll along wide, sandy beaches. Leaving Dana Point Harbor, hike on Doheny State Beach. San Juan Creek flows into the sea. You may be able to wade across, or you can take a short detour along the creek, cross a bridge, and return to the shore.

Families enjoy the calm waters along the initial stretch of Doheny, protected by the harbor's jetty. Volleyball courts were full and surfers were catching three foot waves on the spring morning that we hiked. As we walked further, beyond the sheltered harbor, the waves grew to eight feet, and the number of surfers thinned to only the more experienced.

Doheny State Beach bleeds into Capistrano State Park, to Poche Beach, to San Clemente City Beach. The entire route should be passable, except at high tide. Your way may be blocked by a rip-rap seawall protecting a small beach development beyond Poche Beach. If the way is blocked, leave the beach, carefully cross the Amtrak rails, and walk a short distance along El Camino Real before returning to the shore.

Pass an Amtrak Station at the beginning of San Clemente City Beach. There is a convenient restaurant just inland from the station. Continue along the beach to San Clemente Pier.

Stay in San Clemente and enjoy the inns, restaurants, and

taverns in the neighborhood near the pier. We celebrated the end of a beautiful four day hike at Fisherman's Restaurant which sits at the base of the pier. We started in the bar at sunset with oysters on the half shell, and then moved to the restaurant for delicious fresh

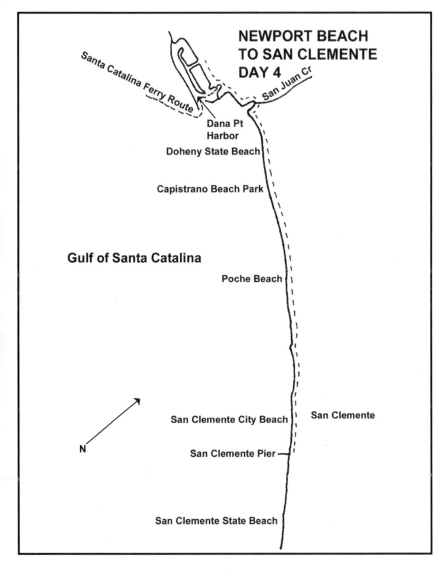

NEWPORT BEACH
TO SAN CLEMENTE
DAY 4

Santa Catalina Ferry Route

San Juan Cr

Dana Pt Harbor

Doheny State Beach

Capistrano Beach Park

Gulf of Santa Catalina

Poche Beach

N

San Clemente City Beach

San Clemente

San Clemente Pier

San Clemente State Beach

calamari and salmon, dining on the open porch, under heat lamps, suspended over the Pacific. Each wave shook the floor as it crashed into the pier.

This 27.3 mile hike is a rich mixture of inviting Southern California beaches and wild rocky shoreline where you share the coast with only shore birds, harbor seals, and dolphins. The beach towns are unique with music, art, history, and fine dining. Take a walkabout and explore the beautiful Orange County Coast, the California Riviera.

THE ROUTE

On this 27.3 mile walkabout, you will hike beautiful sandy beaches separated by rocky shoreline. A few sections are only passable

Crystal Cove Cabins

when the tide is low. Tide schedules are available at ***http://tide-sandcurrents.noaa.gov/tide_predictions.shtm***. Pay attention to the frequent public paths and stairways that lead up from the shore. If your way is blocked, wait for the tide to recede or leave the beach and walk residential streets or the wide shoulder of the highway until you can return to the shore. The hours before and after low tide are the times when you will find the best hiking conditions - wider beaches with firm sand.

All mileages listed for a given day are cumulative.

Day 1:
Newport Beach to Crystal Cove State Park Historic District

Leaving the Newport Pier, hike the beach or paved walking path to Palm St., two blocks before the Balboa Pier, and turn left. .....**1.6 mile**

Walk to the harbor on Palm St. Take the ferry ($1) to Balboa Island. Turn right immediately after leaving the ferry along So. Bay Front. Turn left on Marine Ave. Cross the bridge to the mainland. Turn right on Bayside Dr. ....**2.8 miles**

Walk the sidewalk along Bayside Dr. past the Bahia Corinthian Yacht Club, Balboa Yacht Club, and Harbor Master Coast Guard Station. Turn right and ascend Fernleaf Ave. Turn left on Ocean Blvd. and descend the stairs across from Heliotrope Ave. to Corona del Mar State Beach. ....**4.4 miles**

You can walk the shoreline along sandy beaches and rocky shores to Crystal Cove if the tide is low. Otherwise, continue along Ocean Blvd., turn left on Poppy Ave., walk along Pacific Coast Highway and descend the paved trail just beyond Pelican Point Dr. to Crystal Cove State Beach and Crystal Cove State Park Historic District.
....**total miles 7.2**

Newport Sunset

Day 2:
Crystal Cove State Park Historic District to Laguna Beach

Continue along the beach until it is blocked by steep cliffs. Scramble up the hillside to the Pacific Coast Hwy. just before a 2-story brick and metal structure. ....**1.7 miles**

Walk the wide bike lane and sidewalk along the ocean side of the Pacific Coast Hwy. Turn right on Crescent Bay Dr. .... **3.0 miles**

Take the stairway at the base of Crescent Bay Dr. and a second stairway to Crescent Bay. ....**3.2 miles**

If the tide is low, continue along the shoreline around rocky points and along pocket coves to Laguna Beach. You can climb stairways to the

bluffs from any of the coves if hiking is difficult. If the tide is too high to get past Crescent Bay, return to the steps and turn right on the first street. Follow the street above the coast to Heisler Park. Walk through the park and descend the stairway at the end to Laguna Beach. ....
....**total miles 4.6**

Gardens above Aliso Beach

Day 3: Laguna Beach to Dana Point

Hike along Laguna Beach past Halfway Rock, a rocky point that is easily passable except at high tide, to Cactus Point, a rocky promontory with a tunnel near the surf line. ....**1.3 miles**

Leave the beach just before Cactus Point on stairs with a black railing to Pearl St. Turn right on Ocean Way. Turn left on Moss St. and right on the sidewalk of Pacific Coast Hwy. for a short distance. Turn right on Victoria Dr. At the base of Victoria Dr., before it swings back toward the highway, take the stairs to Victoria Beach. ....**2.2 miles**

Continue on Victoria Beach and round a point at Goff Island, a narrow peninsula ending with a massive rock. ....**2.7 miles**

Crystal Cove

Hike to Aliso Beach along the shoreline and over rock shelves. If the tide is high, take the stairs after Goff Island, and stroll the sidewalk along the bluffs to Aliso Beach. ....**3.3 miles**

Round Aliso Point. This may be impassable if the tide is high. In that case, walk along the Pacific Coast Hwy. from the Aliso Beach parking lot. Otherwise, continue along the beach to the second set of stairs that climb steeply along a tree-lined gully to West St. These stairs are adjacent to a house on the cliffs with tall palm trees. Turn right on

Ruby's at Crystal Cove

Pacific Coast Hwy., walk along the wide bike lane and sidewalk to Ritz Carlton Dr., and turn right. ....**6.1 miles**

Walk past the hotel. Take the stairs at the end of the parking lot to Bluff Park and Salt Creek Beach Park. Hike down the shore beyond a paved roadway that comes down to the beach. The shoreline is blocked by cliffs at Dana Point. Take the stairs about 0.3 miles before Dana Point. ....**7.6 miles**

From the top of the stairs, continue up Ocean Front Lane. Turn right on Dana Strand Road until it ends. Pass through a metal gate, enter Dana Point Preserve and follow the trail to the visitor center. Walk the street from the visitor center and turn right on Cove Rd. to the Dana Point Harbor. .... **total miles 9.5**

Day 4: Dana Point to San Clemente

Return to the shoreline at Doheny State Beach. Detour inland to cross the San Juan Creek on a bridge and return to the beach through the campground. There is a paved bike path at the top of Doheny State Beach to Capistrano Beach, but you can hike the shoreline all the way to the San Clemente Pier. .... **total miles 6.0**

TRANSPORTATION

Flying into Los Angeles

Take a Super Shuttle van from Los Angeles International Airport to Newport Beach Pier. The cost is $46 for the first person and $9 for a second. For information and reservations call 800-258-3826 or try *www.supershuttle.com*. Super Shuttle also serves other L.A. area airports.

Returning from San Clemente to Newport Beach

Visit *www.metro.net* for easy public transportation trip planning. The bus trip from San Clemente Pier to Newport Beach Pier should take 90-120 minutes, and cost $2.

MAPS

The U.S. Geological Survey sells topographical hiking maps and provides free maps you can download. Visit *http://store.usgs.gov* and go to the map locator.

Day 1: Newport Beach OE S Quadrangle and Laguna
       Beach Quadrangle
Day 2: Laguna Beach Quadrangle
Day 3: Laguna Beach Quadrangle and Dana Point Quadrangle
Day 4: Dana Point Quadrangle and San Clemente Quadrangle
Google Maps at *www.maps.google.com* is also a useful tool for viewing the shoreline and roadways adjacent to the shore.

PLACES TO STAY

LODGING COSTS

$ less than $100 | $$ $100-$150 | $$$ $150-$200 | $$$$ more than $200

Newport Beach

Inns near Newport Pier

Bay Shores Peninsula Hotel
1800 W. Balboa Blvd.
800-222-6675
www.thebestinn.com
$$-$$$$

Doryman's Newport Beach Hotel and Inn
2102 W. Oceanfront
949-675-7300
www.dorymansinn.com
$$$$

Newport Beachwalk Hotel
2306 W. Oceanfront Blvd.
800-571-8749
www.newportbeachwalkhotel.com
$$$$

Little Inn by the Bay
29277 Newport Blvd.
800-438-4466
www.littleinnbythebay.com
$$-$$$$

Crystal Cove Park Historic District

Call early to make reservations. Beginning at 8am sharp on the first of each month, the entire seventh months in the future is open for reservations. If you are unable to get a reservation, proceed on to Laguna Beach and combine Days 1 and 2 for an 11.8 mile hike.

Crystal Cove Beach Cottages
35 Crystal Cove
Reservations through www.reserveamerica.com
800-444-7275
www.crystalcovebeachcottages.com
$-$$$$

Laguna Beach

A few of many local inns

Inn at Laguna Beach
211 N. Coast Highway
888-979-9401
www.innatlagunabeach.com
$$$-$$$$

Pacific Edge Hotel
647 S. Coast Highway
949-281-5709
http://www.pacificedgehotel.com
$$-$$$$

Seaside Laguna Inn
1661 S. Coast Highway
949-494-9717
www.seasidelagunainn.com
$$-$$$

Arabella Laguna
506 N. Coast Highway
866-376-5744
www.arabellalaguna.com
$$$-$$$$

Surf and Sand Resort
1555 S. Coast Highway
949-497-4777
www.surfandsandresort.com
$$$$

Dana Point

A few of many local inns

Dana Point Marina Inn
24800 Dana Point Harbor Dr.
800-255-6843
www.danapointmarinainn.com
$-$$$

Blue Lantern Inn
34343 Street of the Blue Lantern
800-950-1236
www.bluelanterninn.com
$$$-$$$$

Doubletree Suites
34402 Pacific Coast Highway
949-661-1100
www.hilton.com
$$-$$$$

Laguna Cliffs Marriott Resort and Spa
25135 Park Lantern
949-661-5000
www.lagunacliffs.com
$$$$

San Clemente

Inns near the San Clemente Pier

Villa Del Mar Inn
612 Avenida Victoria
949-498-5080
www.seahorsesanclemente.com
$$-$$$$

Casa Tropicana Inn at the Pier
610 Avenida Victoria
949-492-1234
www.casatropicana.com
$$$$

Beachcomber Motel
533 Avenida Victoria
949-492-5457
www.beachcombermotel.com
$$-$$$$

Sea Horse Resort
602 Avenida Victoria
949-492-1720
www.seahorsesanclemente.com
$-$$$$

San Clemente Cove Resort
104 S. Alameda Lane
949-492-6666
www.sanclementecove.com
$$$-$$$$

Notes

Notes

5. San Clemente to Oceanside

"We need the tonic of wildness...At the same time that we are earnest to explore and learn all things,

we require that all things be mysterious and unex- plorable, that land and sea be indefinitely wild, un- surveyed and unfathomed by us because unfathom- able. We can never have enough of nature. "

- Henry David Thoreau, *Walden: Or, Life in the Woods*

THIS ONE DAY, 23.8 mile "bridge hike" connects two multi-day walkabouts. There are no inns or restaurants, but the inn-to-inn hiker is rewarded with the longest stretch of accessible un-interrupted, undeveloped shoreline for over 200 miles. Hike miles of plateau between coastal mountains and the sea. Walk through Camp Pendleton where you will experience an active Marine Corps base at two miles an hour. This is a challenging hike. Be sure to bring your driver's license. They will check it as you enter Camp Pendleton.

"In the spring, at the end of the day, you should smell like dirt."

- Margaret Atwood, Bluebeard's Egg

ITINERARY

DAY 1: San Clemente to Oceanside   **23.8**

San Clemente to Oceanside

Most hiking days on the 200 mile Southern California Coast Walk-about are pleasant 5-12 mile strolls. Sleep in, enjoy a leisurely breakfast, hike for 2-6 hours, play on the beach, and celebrate the nightlife of unique and interesting coastal towns. This one is differ-ent, a 23.8 mile hike, a long walk. There are no inns or restaurants between San Clemente and Oceanside, but you will be rewarded for your efforts with miles of beautiful undeveloped beaches, a long hike on the coastal plain, and a rare look at an active military base.

Before you leave San Clemente, you may want to treat yourself to a nice breakfast and to stock up on food and water. These will

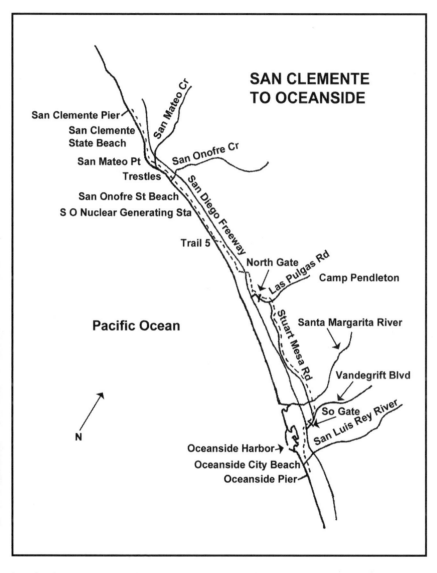

SAN CLEMENTE TO OCEANSIDE

San Mateo Cr

San Clemente Pier

San Clemente State Beach

San Onofre Cr

San Mateo Pt

Trestles

San Onofre St Beach

S O Nuclear Generating Sta

San Diego Freeway

Trail 5

North Gate

Las Pulgas Rd

Camp Pendleton

Pacific Ocean

Stuart Mesa Rd

Santa Margarita River

Vandegrift Blvd

So Gate

San Luis Rey River

Oceanside Harbor

Oceanside City Beach

Oceanside Pier

N

be the last stores and restaurants you will see for the next 23 miles. Head for the shore and walk a beautiful stretch of wide white-sand beach. Amtrak runs at the base of the bluffs. Houses line the cliffs for 1.5 miles until you reach San Clemente State Beach. Here the shore is lined with eighty foot cliffs of deeply eroded sand and sandstone. The next seven miles along San Clemente and San Onofre State Beaches is the longest stretch of accessible, pristine, undeveloped shoreline for over 200 miles from Mexico to the northern tip of L. A. County – no houses, long sandy beaches, rocky shorelines, world class surfing, grand eroded escarpments, wetlands teeming with life, and miles of hiking where you will probably have the beach all to yourself.

Hiking San Clemente State Beach

Rounding San Mateo Point, you cross from Orange County into San Diego County. Only 76 miles to Mexico! The beach becomes steeper with soft sand, so the hiking is a bit slow. This is a favorite surfing area, and on the late March morning that I hiked, surfers crowded the points for the next three miles.

Pass "Trestles," the famous surfing beach named for the railroad bridge that crosses San Mateo Creek. The creek's flow was not powerful enough to reach the Pacific this March, but it formed a wetland, the San Mateo Creek Natural Preserve, filled with tule reeds, cattails, and bird life. Coots and migrating ducks rested in open water; shore birds roamed the water's edge; rabbits streaked in and out of the underbrush. A snowy egret with flowing plumage, looking dignified and vulnerable, stood still, ankle deep. She leaned forward. Then lightning-quick, she pierced the shallows with her long beak and snatched a wriggling frog. Gulp.

Trestles is considered by many to be the preeminent surfing beach in Southern California. Lauded by the Beach Boys in their 1963 hit, "Surfin' USA," it has a contentious history. From World War II to 1971 it was controlled by the Marine Corps. They felt its higher purpose was as a training ground for sea-to-land assaults. Surfers disagreed. They trespassed, were chased, and if caught, arrested and fined. But they persisted. Eventually, the Corps relented and leased the land to the state, who established San Onofre State Beach.

Following a surfer petition campaign, the State Historical Preservation Commission recommended in 2013 that Trestles be listed on the National Registration of Historical Places. Citing its crucial role in "surf culture," they hope to protect Trestles from the threat of development. The Corps opposes the designation fearing civilian oversight and interference.

A hard pack sand road runs along the top of Trestles beach offering a break from soft sand and rocks, a chance to stride out on a flat surface. It continues for 1.3 miles to San Onofre Creek, which forms another lush marshland. You will pass gullies carved by seasonal creeks, but this is the last year-round river for the next 16 miles.

After another short walk on the beach, you reach the campground and parking lot of San Onofre State Beach where there are toilets and vending machines. A hard pack road runs for almost a mile along the top of the beach. Surfers park their cars here to surf and to watch and talk surfing.

The massive San Onofre Nuclear Generating Station looms on the shoreline shortly after the road ends. In 2011, on the western edge of the Pacific, a devastating earthquake and tsunami struck Japan's Fukushima Nuclear Power Plant contaminating the surrounding countryside and poisoning the ocean. It seems unbelievable to find this plant here along the edge of the Pacific, in an active earthquake zone, surrounded by one of the largest population centers in the U.S. The plant was shut down in January 2012 when premature wear was discovered on 3,000 steam generator tubes. In June 2013, Southern California Edison decided to close it permanently. It will take several years before the plant is fully decommissioned and this travesty is removed from the shore.

Pass the power plant on a paved walkway at its base. Then strike out on three miles of pristine shoreline that you will likely have all to yourself. Deeply eroded bluffs, 150 feet high, frame the beach, which changes from sandy to rocky and back again. Shore birds graze along the surf; pelicans glide overhead then tuck their wings and dive for lunch; harbor seals fish just beyond the breakers. I ran into only one other human, an elderly fisherman casting from the shore.

"What are you fishing for?" I asked.

"It's a mess out there today. I guess I'm fishin' for kelp," he said with a cheerful smile as he showed me an empty bucket.

As I walked in blissful solitude, I was reminded of the words of Richard Henry Dana Jr., author of *Two Years Before the Mast*, who sailed from Boston in 1834 to the sparsely populated shores of Mexican California. After months at sea on a small crowded ship,

Uninterrupted Beach

he found himself alone on the shore near San Juan Capistrano.

> *...there was a grandeur in everything around, which gave a solemnity to the scene, a silence and solitariness which affected every part! Not a human being but ourselves for miles, and no sound heard but the pulsations of the great Pacific! And the great steep hill rising like a wall, and cutting us off from all the world but the "world of waters"!*

The rugged cliffs are crowned by chaparral. An occasional

seasonal creek carves a winding course through the bluffs. You will pass one where four stately palms have taken root and guard the arroyo's mouth.

At 8.9 miles there is a lifeguard station marked "trail 5" and an easily recognizable gravel road descending to the beach. There are several small paths leading up from the beach, but this one stands out. Climb the road. There is a bench at the crest of the bluffs. Stop to enjoy the views of uninterrupted beaches both north and south.

Coastal Mountains of Camp Pendleton

Take the trail through coastal chaparral to a parking area, turn right, pass through a gate and enter Camp Pendleton Marine Corp Base. Our trail follows a bike path and lane through the base for the next 11.3 miles, but there is often a gravel shoulder along the paved path that is easier on the feet. The initial bike path is old Highway 101. It is two or three lanes wide and shut off to cars for the next 3.6 miles. There are a few bikers. It travels along the coastal plateau, passes under I-5, and comes to Las Pulgas Road, where you turn left and walk to the camp's official north gate.

A young marine with a buzz cut stood in the middle of the road checking IDs of car and truck drivers as they entered the base. I approached.

"Morning, Sir" he said, "Your driver's license, please."

"Good morning" I said, handing him my license.

"Where are you headed?"

"Oceanside."

"That's a long hike. Where are you coming from?" He sees bicyclists but not many walkers.

"San Clemente. It's a beautiful walk along the beach."

He looked skeptical. "You have plenty of water? You know the route?"

"Yes."

"Alright," he said with an amused smile, "Be safe."

Shortly after the gate, turn right on Stuart Mesa Road and walk the bike lane. The trail turns inland along the broad, grassy littoral terrace between coastal hills and the sea. In early spring, mustard, wild radish, and fennel bloomed in the tall grass.

Camp Pendleton is vast, 130,000 acres. To the east the coastal mountains look dry and unwelcoming. The hike passes a camouflaged encampment. Military vehicles cruise the road. Helicopters fly overhead and land in nearby fields. You get a rare ground level opportunity to look at life on a military base at two miles an hour. Pass a large dining facility, a hospital, and a suburban-like hous-

San Clemente State Beach

ing development where wives meet on quiet lanes with children in strollers. I rarely listen to music while I hike, preferring to tune into the sounds of nature, but on this journey, my MP3 player helped the miles and hours melt away.

The trail leaves the terrace and descends into the Santa Margarita River valley. The quiet stream and wetlands are rich with bird life. Stuart Mesa Road ends at Vandegrift Blvd. where you turn right. Pass the camp's south gate and continue into Oceanside.

The Route will guide you all the way to Oceanside Pier, but most of the inns are near the marina a mile earlier. There are fun bars and restaurants along the marina and easy access to beautiful Oceanside Beach. Relax and enjoy. You have earned it after a unique 23.8 mile walkabout on the Southern California Coast.

Endless Beach

THE ROUTE

Hike the beach on the first 8.9 miles of this walkabout. It should all be passable, even if the tide is high. The hours before and after low tide are the times when you will find the best hiking conditions - wider beaches with firm sand. Tide schedules are available at *http://tidesandcurrents.noaa.gov/tide_predictions.shtm*. This is a long hike, 23.8 miles, with no inns or restaurants. You will need to show your driver's license to enter Camp Pendleton.

All mileages listed for a given day are cumulative.

Day 1: San Clemente Pier to Oceanside Pier

Leaving San Clemente Pier, hike southeast along the shoreline to San Clemente State Park campground. A steep path comes down the bluffs and goes under railroad tracks, connecting campground and beach...**1.5 miles**

(A paved bike path runs along the bluffs. This alternate route can be accessed by walking through the campground and up Avenue Calafia. Turn right on Avenida del Presidente. This 7.4 mile route takes you to

San Mateo Creek Natural Preserve

Camp Pendleton on pavement rather than the beach.)

Continue along the beach to the San Onofre State Beach campground and parking lot. ....**4.1 miles**

Leaving the parking lot, hike the beach to San Onofre Nuclear Generating Station. Walk along the paved walkway at the base of the plant. ....**5.5 miles**

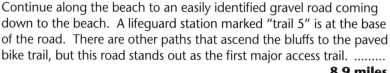
Continue along the beach to an easily identified gravel road coming
down to the beach. A lifeguard station marked "trail 5" is at the base
of the road. There are other paths that ascend the bluffs to the paved
bike trail, but this road stands out as the first major access trail. ....
....**8.9 miles**

Walk up the gravel road, and take the trail to the parking lot. Turn
right, pass through the gate and enter Camp Pendelton. ...**9.5 miles**

Hike the bike path. It passes under I-5 and reaches Las Pulgas Rd.
Turn left to the official north entrance gate of Camp Pendelton. You
will be asked to show a picture I.D. ....**13.1 miles**

Follow the bike lane as it turns right after the entry station onto Stuart
Mesa Rd. This is a long stretch that passes a sign "Camp Pendelton
Edson Range," a medical clinic, Donald Cook Rd., and a suburban-like

Turn Inland at Trail 5 Station

housing sub-division. Descend to Santa Margarita River and to Vande-
grift Blvd. ....**20.8 miles**

Turn right on Vandegrift to the camp's south gate. ....**21.3 miles**

Continue and pass under I-5. Turn left on the Coast Hwy. Cross the
San Luis Rey River. Turn right on Mission Ave. to the Oceanside Pier.
Most of the inns listed in Places to Stay are a mile before the pier, near
the Oceanside Marina. ....**total miles 23.8**

TRANSPORTATION
Flying into Los Angeles
Take a Super Shuttle van from Los Angeles International Airport
to San Clemente. The cost is $59 for the first person and $9 for a
second. For information and reservations call 800-258-3826 or try
www.supershuttle.com. Super Shuttle also serves other L.A. area
airports.

Returning from Oceanside to San Clemente
Take Amtrak's Pacific Surfliner from Oceanside Pier to San Clemente Pier for $11. For information and reservations go to *www.
amtrak.com.* Visit *www.metro.net* for easy public transportation
trip planning. The bus trip from the Oceanside Metrolink Station
to San Clemente Pier should take 90-120 minutes, and cost $2.

MAPS
The U.S. Geological Survey sells topographical hiking maps and
provides free maps you can download. Visit *http://store.usgs.gov*
and go to the map locator. Four USGS maps cover the route.
San Clemente Quadrangle
San Onofre Bluff Quadrangle
Las Pulgas Canyon Quadrangle
Oceanside Quadrangle

Google Maps at *www.maps.google.com* is also a useful tool for viewing the shoreline and roadways adjacent to the shore.

PLACES TO STAY

LODGING COSTS

$ less than $100 | $$ $100-$150 | $$$ $150-$200 | $$$$ more than $200

San Clemente
Inns near the San Clemente Pier

Villa Del Mar Inn
612 Avenida Victoria
949-498-5080
www.seahorsesanclemente.com
$$-$$$$

Casa Tropicana Inn at the Pier
610 Avenida Victoria
949-492-1234
www.casatropicana.com
$$$$

Beachcomber Motel
533 Avenida Victoria
949-492-5457
www.beachcombermotel.com
$$-$$$$

Sea Horse Resort
602 Avenida Victoria
949-492-1720
www.seahorsesanclemente.com
$-$$$$

San Clemente Cove Resort
104 S. Alameda Lane
949-492-6666
www.sanclementecove.com
$$$-$$$$

Oceanside

Wyndham Oceanside Pier Resort
333 No. Myers St.
760-901-1200
www.wyndhamoceansidepier.com
$$-$$$$
Close to Oceanside Pier and downtown
2 night minimum

The following inns are near the marina,
1 mile north of Oceanside Pier

Holiday Inn Oceanside Marina
1401 Carmelo Dr.
760-231-7000
www.holidayinn.com
$$-$$$

Comfort Suites Marina
888 No. Coast Highway
760-722-8880
www.comfortsuites.com
$-$$$

La Quinta Inn
937 No. Coast Highway
760-450-0626
www.laquintaoceanside.com
$-$$$

6. Oceanside to La Jolla

"In the course of a day's walk, you see, there is much variance in the mood. ... He becomes more and more incorporated with the material landscape and the open-air drunkenness grows upon him with great strides, until he posts along the road, and sees everything about him, as in a cheerful dream."

- Robert Louis Stevenson, *Walking Tours*

View of
Point La Jolla

TAKE AN EASY THREE DAY, 28 mile walk along this beautiful stretch of Southern California Coast. You will join scores of beach lovers on lively, popular strands, then hike long, quiet, and secluded beaches. Visit three fun seaside towns with great dining and entertainment. Savor a stroll along miles of pristine beach under the 300 foot cliffs of Torrey Pines State Park. Hike the rugged bluffs of La Jolla Peninsula. Enjoy long days hiking along and swimming in the wild Pacific.

"Natural Selection has designed us – from the structure of our brain-cells to the structure of our big toe – for a career of seasonal journeys on foot..."

- Bruce Chatwin, The Songlines

ITINERARY

DAY 1: Oceanside Marina to South Carlsbad State Beach		**7.7**
DAY 2: South Carlsbad State Beach to Del Mar		**11.9**
DAY 3: Del Mar to La Jolla		**8.4**
TOTAL MILEAGE		**28.0**

Day 1: Oceanside Marina To South Carlsbad State Beach

Enjoy Oceanside before you start this 28-mile, three-day hike with a stroll along the marina to the beach. Shops and restaurants line the walkway. Stop at Lighthouse Oyster Bar and Grill for happy hour or dine on grilled fish from the second story deck overlooking the harbor crowded with pleasure craft, fishing boats, kayaks, and jet skis.

My wife, Heidi, and I hiked this walkabout in late June. It is

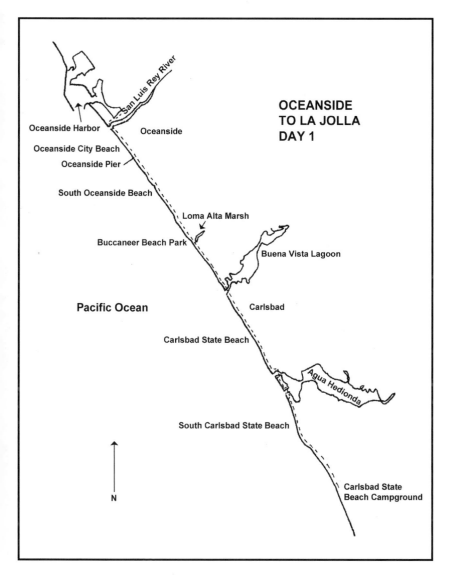

OCEANSIDE
TO LA JOLLA
DAY 1

San Luis Rey River

Oceanside Harbor

Oceanside

Oceanside City Beach

Oceanside Pier

South Oceanside Beach

Loma Alta Marsh

Buccaneer Beach Park

Buena Vista Lagoon

Pacific Ocean

Carlsbad

Carlsbad State Beach

Agua Hedionda

South Carlsbad State Beach

N

Carlsbad State
Beach Campground

beautiful any time of year, but early summer may be the best. The weather was perfect – daytime highs in the low 70s, water temperatures in the high 60s, and balmy short-sleeve evenings. It was one of the longest days of the year when we dined on the Lighthouse's deck on oysters on the half shell, fresh grilled mahi mahi, and sea bass. The sun set far to the north, over the harbor and into the cobalt blue Pacific. Wisps of clouds on the horizon and the vapors of jet contrails glowed pink and orange as the brightest stars emerged.

This entire walkabout can be hiked along the beach, if the tide is not high, with only a few detours to cross bridges over the outlets of lagoons. When the tide is in, you may need to walk residential streets or the sidewalk or bike lane along Pacific Coast Highway for short sections. There are frequent paths and public stairs for leaving the beach and returning if your passage is blocked. See *http:// tidesandcurrents.noaa.gov/tide_predictions.shtm* for tide charts.

Cross San Luis Rey River on Pacific St. Bridge or wade across at the beach. You will find a flat and firm surface, ideal for hiking. The best times for beach hiking are the hours before and after low tide. This perfect hiking surface continues for the full three days of this walkabout.

Beach goers arrive early on summer mornings. They cluster around the Oceanside Pier – surfers, boogie boarders, distance swimmers, sun bathers, Frisbee throwers, power and dog walkers. People gather around spots with easy access by car, leaving more distant sections nearly empty. You will alternate between delightful people watching near parking areas and then strolling quiet beaches that you will have almost to yourself.

Houses line Oceanside Beach until a small break at Buccaneer Beach Park where Loma Alta Marsh connects to the sea, and then a longer break at Buena Vista Lagoon. The lagoons on this stretch of the Pacific reach deep into the coastal plain, breathing in and out twice a day with the tides. They are a crucial refuge for migrating birds, native plant species, and humans, their existence threatened by development and valiantly defended by citizens.

This was the land of the Luiseño. They lived along this Pacific shoreline and inland to the San Jacinto Mountains for over 2,000 years. The bountiful ocean, lush wetlands, and verdant San Luis Rey River Valley provided an abundance of food and building materials. The Spanish arrived in 1769 and coveted this land. Many missions struggled to feed themselves, but Mission San Luis Rey de Francia, established in 1789, thrived.

Carlsbad State Beach

Eroded bluffs rise to forty feet along Carlsbad State Beach and houses are infrequent. The north end of the long beach is broad. Two paved pathways border the beach, one on the bluffs and one at beach level. Leave the shore twice to walk bridges over surging Agua Hedionda Lagoon. The beach narrows south of the lagoon. We started hiking at low tide. There was no trouble completing this seven mile stretch of shore, but an hour after we arrived, South Carlsbad State Beach disappeared under the rising tide. No problem, there are several stairways and paths to the bluff trails.

If you would like to shorten this day by 2.5 miles, and lengthen the second day, stop at the inns near Carlsbad Village. Please see Places to Stay. Otherwise, Hilton Garden Inn has the most convenient location, above South Carlsbad State Beach, 0.5 miles before the state campground. From the beach, you can see the campground perched on the cliffs. Dine at the hotel, or ride their free shuttle to the village restaurants. If you have the energy, enjoy an evening stroll 2.0 miles north of the Hilton to Vigilucci's Seafood and Steakhouse. You will be rewarded with delicately prepared seafood, hearty pastas, or succulent steaks served to you on their terrace overlooking the Pacific and setting sun. Ask your innkeeper to make a reservation for a table with a view.

Day 2: South Carlsbad State Beach to Del Mar

Ready for another day of strolling the shoreline of the beautiful Pacific? This 11.9 mile day continues the journey. High and low tides occur about one hour later than the previous day. Time the tides well, and you can hike this entire section with only short detours to cross bridges over the outlets of lagoons.

We started in the early morning, two hours before low tide. A handful of surfers, stand up paddle boarders, and a kayaker rode gentle three foot swells. The flat water, stretching to the horizon, was suddenly alive with a pod of dolphins. Black dorsal fins rose and fell with each breath. They circled to feed and the sea roiled just beyond the breakers as they darted and dove. One leaped, slapping the surface with her tail. Seagulls swooped in, hoping for scraps. Then the dolphins swam slowly south at our pace, occasionally stopping to feed. We traveled together, along the shoreline,

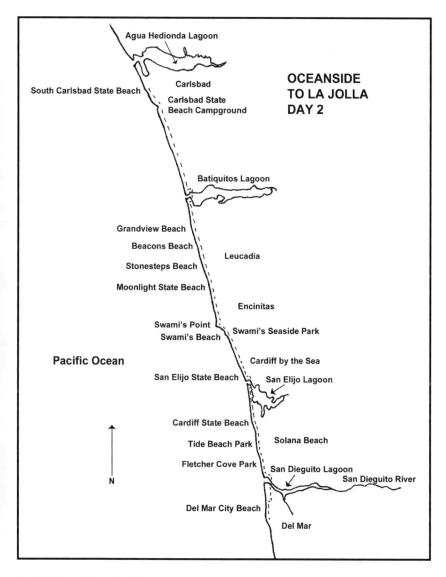

OCEANSIDE
TO LA JOLLA
DAY 2

Agua Hedionda Lagoon

Carlsbad

South Carlsbad State Beach

Carlsbad State
Beach Campground

Batiquitos Lagoon

Grandview Beach

Beacons Beach

Leucadia

Stonesteps Beach

Moonlight State Beach

Encinitas

Swami's Point

Swami's Beach

Swami's Seaside Park

Pacific Ocean

Cardiff by the Sea

San Elijo State Beach

San Elijo Lagoon

Cardiff State Beach

Tide Beach Park

Solana Beach

Fletcher Cove Park

San Dieguito Lagoon

San Dieguito River

N

Del Mar City Beach

Del Mar

for half an hour before they disappeared.

Continue hiking the long Carlsbad State Beach. Jog around
the outlet of Batiquitos Lagoon, and hike a series of beaches along
Leucadia and Encinitas – Grandview Beach, Beacons Beach, Ston-

Carlsbad Sunrise

esteps Beach and Moonlight State Beach. Cliffs rise to 60 feet south of Moonlight State Beach, and houses cling to the edge. Some patios suspend over the eroded abyss waiting the slow passage of time or a quick jolt from the next big one. Vibrant naturalized gardens of ice plant, violet lantana, purple sea foam, and prickly pear cactus, along with escaped exotics – wild red roses and scarlet bougainvillea – spill down the steep escarpment.

In late June, scores of kids swarmed Moonlight State Beach for summer camps – volleyball, surfing, ocean safety, junior life guards, and YMCA boot camp. They wore matching t-shirts so their instructors could track them. "Run to the ocean and back." They dashed, trying to win the race. "Now ten pushups." The kids dropped and gave 'em ten, collapsing in giggles and exhaustion.

Round Swami's Point, the first distinct promontory on this day's hike. It is named for Paramahansa Yogananda. Built in 1936, his Self Realization Fellowship retreat and hermitage perches on the bluffs. The Fellowship has over 500 meditation centers, ashrams, retreats, and temples around the world teaching scientific methods of concentration and meditation to reach a direct experience of God. Paramahansa Yogananda wrote Autobiography of a Yogi at this hermitage during his last years. His friend, sitar master Ravi Shankar, preformed his first U.S. concert here in 1957. George Harrison spent time here and donated the proceeds from the 2002 reissue of "My Sweet Lord" to the Fellowship.

Hungry? Climb the steps beyond the point and turn left passing the beautiful gardens of the hermitage. Cross the street to Swami's Café for breakfast or lunch. Try the acai bowl for an energizing shot of fruit and granola or settle in for a hearty plate of omelet and home fries.

Continue hiking along Swami's Beach and San Elijo State Beach to Cardiff State Beach passing San Elijo Lagoon. Shore birds were much less common in late June than in the spring, but they gathered at the mouth of the lagoon. Marbled godwits foraged along the shore on stilt-like legs, long curved beaks piercing the wet sand for crustaceans, larvae, worms, and mollusks. Snowy egrets with long feathers, almost impossibly white, waded in the surf on tall thin legs, knees bending backwards, head bobbing with each step, ready to strike.

Pass Solana Beach's Tide Beach Park and Fletcher Cove Park. Take a brief detour around San Dieguito Lagoon. The Del Mar Racetrack stands across the marsh. Americans were crazy about horse racing in the 1930s and 40s. The Del Mar track became a playground for the stars of Hollywood. On its opening day in

1937, Bing Crosby greeted fans as they entered the gate. Its most famous race took place on August 12, 1938, the first thoroughbred race broadcast nationwide by radio. Legendary Seabiscuit faced off against the Argentinian steed, Ligaroti, in a winner-take-all contest for the phenomenal purse of $25,000. Seabiscuit broke fast out of the gate and took the lead. Ligarote caught him on the backstretch and briefly surged ahead. They battled down the stretch. America's hero, Seabiscuit, won by a nose.

Del Mar City Beach

Enter Del Mar's popular main beach. People are playing horseshoes, Frisbee, volleyball, whiffle ball golf. They are surfing, boogie boarding, body surfing, sunbathing, and picnicking. Kids with buckets and shovels are building elaborate sand castles. It is a people watching feast.

After two good days of hiking, you may want to take a rest day in Del Mar. Enjoy the beautiful beach and the many restaurants and watering holes. There are several elegant inns, but I suggest Del Mar Motel on the Beach, a throwback to 1970s Southern California motel design, nothing fancy, but step out of your room and right onto the beach. They will provide you with beach towels, chairs, umbrellas, and boogie boards.

Day 3: Del Mar to La Jolla

A light haze was just starting to burn off when we hit the beach for the final leg of this walkabout. Deeply eroded cliffs bordering the beach reach 60 feet. Another pod of a dozen dolphins swam with us, trolling for breakfast.

The cliffs recede at Los Peñasquitos Lagoon. This is the start of Torrey Pines State Beach. Passing the lagoon, the cliffs soon soar to 300 feet topped by stately trees, Torrey pines. You may want to hike the winding park road and climb to the visitor center and museum, an adobe building constructed in 1923. It is worth a visit, and will give you a chance to get a close up view of the trees. They are the rarest native pine tree in the new world, growing only here in the state reserve, in neighboring yards up to Del Mar, and on Santa Rosa Island, 170 miles to the northwest off the coast of Santa Barbara. Once thriving throughout much of Southern California, their range diminished 11,000 years ago after the last ice age. Battered and twisted on the windy western side of the reserve, they stand tall and full, up to 60 feet, on the protected leeward side. Their needles grow to ten inches in groups of five, and their roots spread 200 feet to find moisture in a land that receives only ten inches of rain a year.

The Beach Trail from the visitor center hikes through chaparral

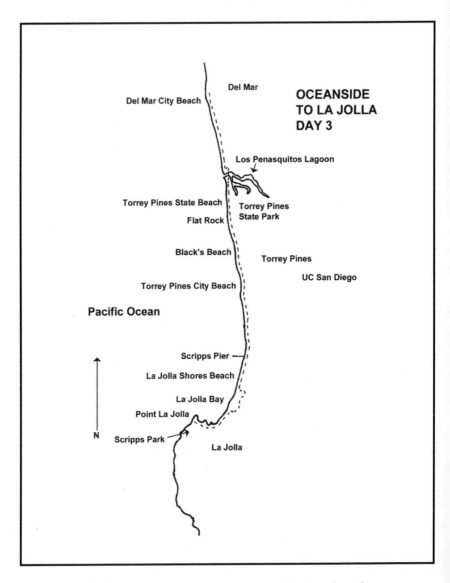

**OCEANSIDE
TO LA JOLLA
DAY 3**

Del Mar

Del Mar City Beach

Los Penasquitos Lagoon

Torrey Pines State Beach

Torrey Pines
State Park

Flat Rock

Black's Beach

Torrey Pines

UC San Diego

Torrey Pines City Beach

Pacific Ocean

Scripps Pier

La Jolla Shores Beach

La Jolla Bay

Point La Jolla

Scripps Park

N

La Jolla

and sandy bluffs, returning to the shore at Flat Rock. This is one of the most isolated and serene beaches on the Southern California Coast. Rain has cut deep arroyos through 300 foot sandstone escarpments. Hang gliders launch from cliffs and float on updrafts.

The wide, uninterrupted beach stretches for miles. Millions live nearby, but one must be willing to hike to enjoy this splendor.

Continue on Black's Beach, a low key clothing-optional stretch. The cliffs are now dotted with houses. One house, a concrete cylinder sits alone on the beach, at the base of the cliffs, with a tramway to the top. It looks absolutely out of place and like it once belonged to George J. Jetson.

Torrey Pines City Beach ends with a rocky promontory, the only section that requires some bouldering along this three-day walkabout. Families were tide pooling among the rocks when we

Torrey Pines City Beach

passed, 1.5 hours after low tide. It would be easily passable for at least another two hours. If your passage is blocked, return a short distance to the path leading up the bluffs, and follow The Route back to the beach.

Pass by Scripps Institution of Oceanography and Scripps Pier.

La Jolla Bay

Stroll through very popular La Jolla Shores Beach. And here you can swim with the sharks. Leopard sharks swarm to these waters between June and December, their numbers peaking in August and September. They are cold blooded, and pregnant females come to the warm shallows to help incubate their developing embryos. Up to five feet long, leopard sharks have tiny mouths for feeding on small fish, shrimp, and crustaceans.

They are not aggressive and a bit shy. Kayakers and snorkelers float, watching dozens of sharks swimming below. Waders stand still while the mothers-to-be gracefully swim around their legs.

Leaving La Jolla Shores Beach, follow The Route for the path through the neighborhood and along the bluffs above La Jolla Bay. You are hiking one of the most beautiful sections of the Southern

California Coast, La Jolla Peninsula, a rugged coastline with sheer cliffs, pocket coves, and inviting beaches. Sea lions lounge on the rocks below. Snorkelers, long distance swimmers, stand up paddle boarders, and kayakers ply the clear waters of La Jolla Bay and Cove.

This is another spot to spend an extra day, a friendly town with great restaurants, inns, and shopping. The rocky peninsula is rich with hidden coves and beaches to explore. It is a great place to end a three-day immersion in the lifestyle and beauty of the Southern California Coast.

THE ROUTE

The entire route of this three-day walkabout is passable at lower

Summer Camp

Del Mar Motel

tides. If your passage is blocked by high tides, take one of the frequent paths or public stairs to briefly walk residential streets and return to the beach. Tide schedules are available at *http://tidesandcurrents.noaa.gov/tide_predictions.shtml*.

All mileages listed for a given day are cumulative.

Day 1: Oceanside Marina to South Carlsbad State Beach

Leaving Oceanside Marina, either walk to the ocean and wade across the San Luis Rey River or cross Pacific St. bridge and take the first right on No. Coast Village to the beach and to Oceanside Pier. ..**1.0 miles**

Houses line the beach. You will see a small break in the houses at Buccaneer Beach Park and Loma Alta Marsh. ....**3.6 miles**

To Buena Vista Lagoon ....**4.6 miles**

Hike to Agua Hedionda Lagoon. Cross two bridges over the lagoon's outlets. ....**5.7 miles**

To South Carlsbad State Beach. The state beach campground can be seen on the bluff. (Please see Places to Stay. Inns are spread out along Carlsbad State Beach.)................................. **total miles 7.7**

Day 2: South Carlsbad State Beach to Del Mar

Hike the beach to Batiquitos Lagoon. ....**2.4 miles**

To Moonlight State Beach. ....**5.4 miles**

Round Swami's Point to Swami's Beach. ....**6.5 miles**

Swami's

To San Elijo Lagoon. ....**7.9 miles**

To San Dieguito Lagoon. ....**10.8 miles**

Cross the lagoon on the bridge, turn right on 29th St., return to the shore and Del Mar City Beach. ....**total miles 11.9**

Day 3: Del Mar to La Jolla

From Del Mar City Beach, hike to the Torrey Pines State Beach parking area and Los Peñasquitos Lagoon. ....**2.0 miles**

To Flat Rock. ....**3.4 miles**

To Scripps Pier. ....**6.4 miles**

Torrey Pine

Passage may be blocked by a rocky promontory just north of Scripps Pier if the tide is high. Return to the major trail ascending the bluffs, and hike to the parking area. Turn right on La Jolla Farms Rd., right on La Jolla Shores Dr., and return to the beach.

To La Jolla Shores Beach. .... **7.5 miles**

Hike to the very end of La Jolla Shores Beach and take a narrow pathway at the end of a long condominium complex. Turn right on Spindrift, right on Torrey Pines Rd., and right on Coastwalk. Hike the path along the cliffs above La Jolla Bay to La Jolla Cove. Downtown La Jolla is one block inland. .... **total miles 8.4**

TRANSPORTATION

Flying into San Diego

Take a Super Shuttle van from San Diego Airport to Oceanside. The cost is $55 for the first person and $9 for a second. For information and reservations call 800-258-3826 or try *www.supershuttle.com*. Super Shuttle also serves L.A. area airports.

Returning from La Jolla to Oceanside

Take Amtrak's Pacific Surfliner from the Solana Beach Station to Oceanside Pier for $11. For information and reservations go to *www.amtrak.com*. To reach the Solana Beach Station from La Jolla, visit *www.transit.511sd.com* for easy public transportation trip planning. The bus trip from La Jolla to Solana Beach Station should take 90 minutes, and cost $2.25. A taxi from La Jolla to Solana Beach Station is faster and should cost around $45. Try Leucadia Transportation at 858-625-1200 or Martina Transportation at 858-401-0877.

MAPS

The U.S. Geological Survey sells topographical hiking maps and provides free maps you can download. Visit *http://store.usgs.gov* and go to the map locator.

Day 1: Oceanside Quadrangle, San Luis Rey Quadrangle, and En cinitas Quadrangle

Day 2: Encinitas Quadrangle and Del Mar OE W Quadrangle

Day 3: Del Mar OE W Quadrangle and La Jolla OE W Quadrangle

Google Maps at *www.maps.google.com* is also a useful tool for viewing the shoreline and roadways adjacent to the shore.

PLACES TO STAY

LODGING COSTS

$ less than $100 | $$ $100-$150 | $$$ $150-$200 | $$$$ more than $200

Oceanside

Wyndham Oceanside Pier Resort
333 No. Myers St.
760-901-1200
www.wyndhamoceansidepier.com
$$-$$$$
Close to Oceanside Pier and downtown
2-night minimum

The following inns are near the marina,
1 mile north of Oceanside Pier

Holiday Inn Oceanside Marina
1401 Carmelo Dr.
760-231-7000
www.holidayinn.com
$$-$$$

Comfort Suites Marina
888 No. Coast Highway
760-722-8880
www.comfortsuites.com
$-$$$

La Quinta Inn
937 No. Coast Highway
760-450-0626
www.laquintaoceanside.com
$-$$$

Carlsbad State Beach
These inns are spread out above the state beach

Hilton Garden Inn Carlsbad Beach
6450 Carlsbad Blvd.
855-476-0800
www.hiltongardeninncarlsbad.com
$$-$$$$
0.5 miles north of state park campground

Surf Motel
3136 Carlsbad Blvd.
800-308-5457
www.surfmotelcarlsbad.com
$-$$
0.7 miles south of Buena Vista Lagoon

Tamarack Beach Resort
3200 Carlsbad Blvd.
760-729-3500
www.tamarackresort.com
$$-$$$$
0.7 miles south of Buena Vista Lagoon

Carlsbad Seapointe Resort
6400 Surfside Lane
760-603-1700
www.carlsbadseapointe.com
$$$-$$$$
0.5 miles south of state park campground

Beach Terrace Inn
2775 Ocean St.
800-433-5415
www.beachterraceinn.com
$$$-$$$$
0.5 miles south of Buena Vista Lagoon

Carlsbad Inn Beach Resort
3075 Carlsbad Blvd.
760-434-7020
www.carlsbadinn.com
$$$-$$$$
0.6 miles south of Buena Vista Lagoon

Del Mar

Del Mar Motel on the Beach
1702 Coast Blvd.
800-223-8449
www.delmarmotelonthebeach.com
$$-$$$$

Clarion Inn
720 Camino Del Mar
858-755-9765
www.clarionhotel.com
$$-$$$$

Hotel Indigo
710 Camino Del Mar
877-270-1392
www.hotelindigo.com
$$-$$$

Les Artistes Inn
944 Camino Del Mar
858-755-4646
www.lesartistesinn.com
$$-$$$$

La Jolla
These are a few of the many places to stay

Inn by the Sea Best Western Plus
7830 Fay Ave.
858-459-4461
www.bestwestern.com
$$-$$$$

Empress Hotel
7766 Fay Ave.
858-454-3001
www.empress-hotel.com
$$-$$$$

La Valencia Hotel
1132 Prospect St.
858-454-0771
www.lavalencia.com
$$$$

La Jolla Cove Suites
1155 Coast Blvd.
858-459-2621
www.lajollacove.com
$$-$$$$

Notes

7. La Jolla to Mexico

"My God is the God of Walkers. If you walk hard enough, you probably don't need any other god."

- Bruce Chatwin, In Patagoni

*View of
Imperial Beach*

THIS IS THE FINAL LEG of a 200 mile inn-to-inn hiking adventure from north L.A. County to the border with Mexico. You will hike rugged, rocky coastlines and sublime swimming beaches on this 32-mile, five-day walk. Pass through working class seaside villages and elegant upscale towns, both offering great cuisine, interesting inns, and always – the wild Pacific. Enjoy wildlife preserves teeming with birdlife and miles of solitude strolling long beaches. Hike inn-to-inn along the southwest corner of the continental U.S.A.

> *"One cannot think well, love well, sleep well, if one has not dined well."*
>
> *- Virginia Woolf, A Room of One's Own*

ITINERARY

DAY 1: La Jolla to Crystal Pier, Pacific Beach	**5.1**
DAY 2: Crystal Pier, Pacific Beach to Shelter Island Yacht Basin	**8.5**
DAY 3: Shelter Island Yacht Basin to Coronado Village	**6.8**
DAY 4: Coronado Village to Imperial Beach Municipal Pier	**8.1**
DAY 5: Imperial Beach Municipal Pier to U.S./Mexico Border	**3.3**
TOTAL MILEAGE	**31.8**

Day 1: La Jolla to Crystal Pier, Pacific Beach

Start this five-day, 32-mile journey in La Jolla, "the jewel." It is perched on a rugged promontory and separated from the dense urban and freeway life of L.A. and San Diego. Walk to Point La Jolla, and cast your gaze to the north. A long arc of shoreline stretches from the La Jolla headlands to Palos Verdes Peninsula. To the south are crystal clear lagoons and pocket beaches. Sea lions and

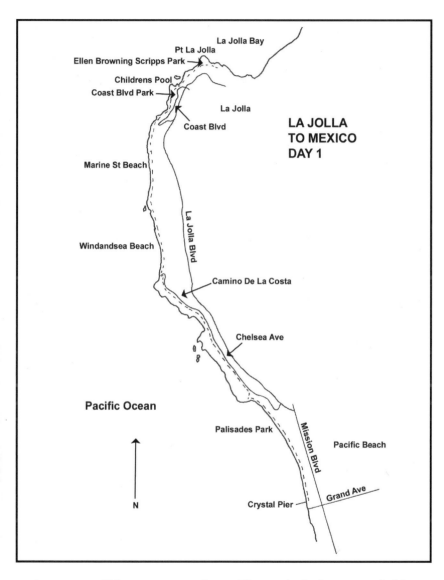

La Jolla Bay
Pt La Jolla
Ellen Browning Scripps Park
Childrens Pool
Coast Blvd Park
Coast Blvd
La Jolla

**LA JOLLA
TO MEXICO
DAY 1**

Marine St Beach

La Jolla Blvd

Windandsea Beach

Camino De La Costa

Chelsea Ave

Pacific Ocean

Palisades Park

Mission Blvd

Pacific Beach

Grand Ave

Crystal Pier

N

seals rest on offshore outcroppings. Flat rock shelves pounded by relentless waves are ideal for hiking. All this greets you as you set out on a hike to the border.

My friend, Scott, and I hiked this walkabout in late July. We

Harbor Seals on Children's Beach

started with a day exploring La Jolla – watching the world go by over fish tacos and beers from a sidewalk table at Jose's Courtroom on Prospect St. and swimming in the warm waters of La Jolla Cove. That evening, the Prospect Bar and Grill treated us to live music, a salsa lesson, basil salmon, and grilled ahi.

Temperatures were in the high 60s at dawn. When the thin morning fog burned off, they rose to the mid-70s. Water temperatures were also in the high 60s. It is an ideal season to hike the Southern California Coast. Take a break from hiking with a dive into the Pacific. There are countless opportunities.

Start your journey at Ellen Browning Scripps Park. In the early morning it comes alive with gulls, joggers, dog walkers, and families playing on the lush grass. The park overlooks the protected waters of La Jolla Underwater Park and Ecological Reserve - 6,000 acres, extending north to Torrey Pines. Its two underwater gorges, La Jolla Canyon and Scripps Canyon, plunge deep into the ocean floor creating a rich environment for marine life. Migrating whales feed close to shore. Dolphins, sea lions, seals, leopard sharks, shovel-nose guitarfish, and garibaldi damselfish thrive in the clear waters. Explore the reserve up close by going to *www.sandiegobikeandkayaktours.com* for snorkel and kayak rentals.

Hike south from Scripps Park on coastal bluffs past Children's Pool, a beach sheltered by a seawall and a favorite gathering spot for harbor seals, who appear to have taken over from the children.

La Jolla Shoreline

Dozens of the pinnipeds crowded the beach on the morning we walked, lying near the water's edge, all facing out to sea.

Drop down to a coastal sandstone terrace, weathered and worn smooth by the forces of wind, rain, and sea. Houses line the bluffs above the rock shelves, older and more modest than the newer mansions that crowd most of the prime real estate along this coast. They face the sea with verdant lawns, verandas, and picture windows. Old stately Mexican fan palms sway in the breeze on slender sixty foot trunks, crowned with cascading fronds.

Windandsea Beach

Terraces give way to Marine St. Beach and then long, crescent Windandsea Beach. Passage along the shore is blocked beyond Windandsea Beach. Follow The Route through the seaside neighborhoods of La Jolla. Stroll past older, well established gardens rich with red and white roses, salmon and purple bougainvillea, orange lantana, and blue agapanthus. Stop to enjoy overlooks and small parks with stairs down to rocky beaches.

It was a calm day when we walked, and a few surfers caught 2-3 foot waves off rocky points. They were joined by kayakers and stand up paddle boarders. Cormorants, gulls, and harbor seals rested on offshore rocks.

Leave the neighborhood at 4.1 miles, and hike the shore of Palisades Park and Pacific Beach to Crystal Pier. In summer, the beach teems with surfers and sun worshippers. As you approach the pier, walk the sand or the paved Ocean Front Walk. The mood is mellow as patrons lounge in sidewalk restaurants and cafes, watching the passing scene along the strand – bikers, skaters, joggers, and strollers. There are many restaurants, bars, and inns along the beach. Lodging ranges from the Banana Bungalow, a hostel that costs as low as $18 a night, to the Crystal Pier Hotel and Cottages. Their cottages line the private pier and will set you back $175 or more. It is said that you can cast a line from your cottage window and catch dinner.

Day 2: Crystal Pier, Pacific Beach to Shelter Island Yacht Basin

Walk south along the flat, firm beach, or stroll Ocean Front Walk. Stop for breakfast at a sidewalk café, and watch the fascinating early morning promenade.

You reach Belmont Park at 1.7 miles. It is easy to identify by the street lights that now line Ocean Front Walk and the old fashioned wooden roller coaster, the Giant Dipper, which etches the skyline. Turn inland through Mission Bay Park, surrounding Mission Bay. With over 4,200 acres of land and saltwater bays, it is the largest man-made aquatic park in the U.S.

Europeans stumbled upon this bay in 1542 when it was ringed by tidal marshes and a labyrinth of mudflats. Juan Rodrigues

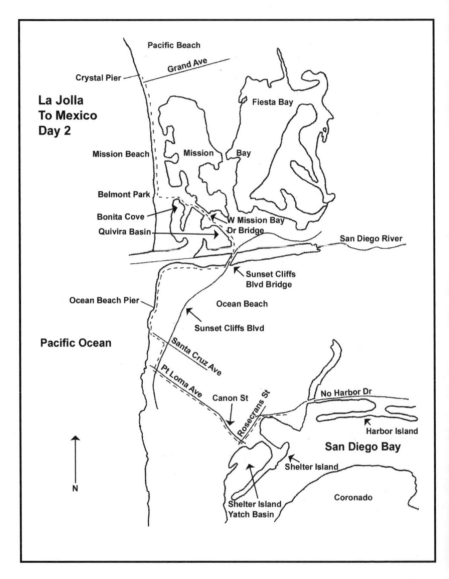

Cabrillo was commissioned by the Viceroy of New Spain to lead
an expedition to explore the Pacific Coast, find a route to China,
and discover the mythical Strait of Anián, the Northwest Passage
connecting Hudson Bay and the Pacific. On September 28, his two

ships, San Salvador and Victoria, sailed into San Diego Bay.

Cabrillo sent a small party ashore to find good water to replenish the ship's dwindling supplies. They followed the bed of the San Diego River, but the rainy season would not come for another month, and the river was dry. As darkness descended, they reached the shoreline of a great bay and looked in vain for the ships. After camping that night, they were rescued by a search party and guided

Crystal Pier Cottages

back. The wayward explorers had found a second bay north of San Diego Bay, which they named "False Bay." Many early mariners mistook the entrance to False Bay, now called Mission Bay, for the mouth of San Diego Bay.

Follow The Route, and stroll through the park's grassy fields planted with dignified palms. Families enjoy picnics and kids romp in the warm, calm waters. Pass yachts anchored in Mariners Basin. Cross the main channel of Mission Bay on West Mission Bay Dr. Bridge, and walk along Quivira Basin Yacht Harbor. Small fishing craft, cigarette boats, and luxury yachts crowd the docks. Cross San Diego River on Sunset Cliffs Blvd., and follow the bike path along the river to Ocean Beach.

Marbled Godwits on Pacific Beach

This was not always the path of the San Diego River. It starts high in the Cuyamaca Mountains and flows 52 miles to the Pacific. Floods throughout history shifted the river's course, and it discharged sometimes into San Diego Bay and other times into False Bay. When the first settlers arrived in the late 18th century, the river flowed into False Bay. Flooding in the 1820s, most likely the violent storms in the winter of 1824-25, sent it careening across the floodplain to empty into San Diego Bay. In 1852, fearing that the valuable harbor would silt up, the U.S. Army Corp of Engineers built a dike that sent the river back to False Bay. Two years later, the dike failed. In 1877 the city erected a permanent dam and channeled the river to its present course, flowing into the ocean adjacent to Mission Bay.

Ocean Beach was packed on the July morning of our journey. Scores of surfers sat astride their boards, searching for a modest breaker in the calm waters.

Walk the concrete path under the base of Ocean Beach Pier to a set of stairs that leads to a beautiful series of worn rock shelves at the base of the bluffs. A coastal terrace formed by waves and uplifted from the ancient seabed, it is an ideal hiking surface. Surges crash against its outer edge sending cascades of spray high into the air and carving sandy pocket beaches. Small crabs scurry between tide pools.

Rock Shelves South of Ocean Beach

Mission Bay

Climb the first stairway, and follow The Route through the neighborhood. The Point Loma Beach Café at the corner of Sunset Cliffs Blvd. and Pt. Loma Ave. is a good place to stop for lunch or a smoothie before ascending Pt. Loma Ave. over the spine of Point Loma, the narrow peninsula that separates Mission and San Diego Bays. Houses are older, smaller, and more time-worn near the coast in this working class community. As you climb, lots expand and the houses grow larger.

Reaching the crest, a view unfolds of San Diego Bay, the sky-scrapers of downtown San Diego backed by the high peaks of the Laguna Mountains, and the gracefully arcing San Diego-Coronado Bay Bridge. Looking south, in the distance on a clear day, you can catch your first glimpse of the hills of Mexico.

Descend to the top of San Diego Bay and Shelter Island Yacht Basin. You have entered the sphere of urban San Diego. There are several hotels, restaurants, and watering holes around the yacht basin. Try Jimmy's Famous American Tavern for drinks or a dinner of comfort food – burgers, steaks, and seafood with a view. If you yearn for excellent sushi, try Umi Sushi. We sat at the bar and ordered a variety of nigiri sushi and rolls. The chefs, one from Thailand and the other Korea, took a fondness to us and served up tastes of delicious delicacies until we could eat no more. We departed, sated, and strolled to our hotel in the balmy San Diego evening.

Day 3: Shelter Island Yacht Basin to Coronado Village

Day three hikes along the rim of San Diego Bay. From the north shore, you see yacht marinas, the downtown skyline, and a wide crescent channel, the outlet to the Pacific. Follow the bike path and sidewalk past Point Loma Naval Base to Harbor Island and Spanish Landing Park.

When Cabrillo visited San Diego Bay in 1542, he named it San Miguel and claimed the land for the Spanish Crown. It took sixty years for the next Europeans to sail into the sheltered harbor. In 1602, Sebastián Vizcaíno led an expedition mapping the coast of Alta California. His two small ships entered the bay in November and anchored in the lee of Point Loma. His crew camped near the Kumeyaay village of Nipaguay and celebrated mass on the feast day of San Diego de Alcalá. He renamed the bay.

Native people have lived in this land for at least 9,600 years, and the Kumeyaay for at least 1,000. There is no record of the impact on the Kumeyaay from the first two European expeditions. Perhaps new diseases took their toll. The next visitors came 167 years later, in 1769. This time, they came to stay. Gaspar de Por-

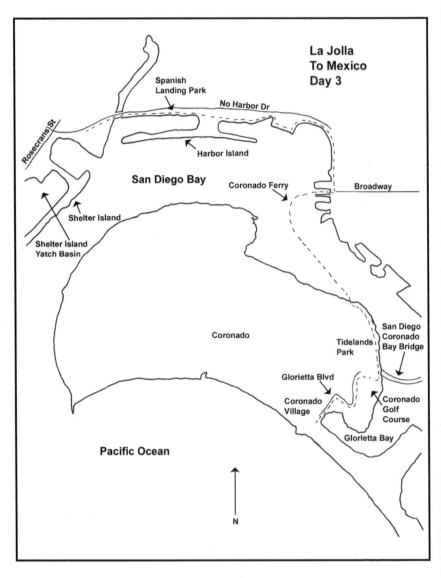

La Jolla
To Mexico
Day 3

Spanish Landing Park

No Harbor Dr

Rosecrans St

Harbor Island

San Diego Bay

Coronado Ferry

Broadway

Shelter Island

Shelter Island Yatch Basin

Coronado

Tidelands Park

San Diego Coronado Bay Bridge

Glorietta Blvd

Coronado Village

Coronado Golf Course

Glorietta Bay

Pacific Ocean

N

tolá and Father Junípero Serra led a land expedition from Mexico. They met the rest of their forces, a sea expedition, here at Spanish Landing.

The land and sea were bountiful. It is estimated that 20,000

Kumeyaay and Luiseño lived in the territory between Oceanside, Northern Baja California, and the Colorado River. They practiced agriculture, planting gardens of medicinal plants and defending their villages with stands of cactus and brambles. They used fire management, burning dried grasslands and broadcasting seeds to produce maize and other crops.

On July 16, 1769, Serra established the Mission San Diego de Alcalá, the first of 21 California missions. A deeply religious and ambitious man, he punished himself to purify his spirit, wearing sackcloth spiked with bristles and broken wire under friar's robes. He punctuated his sermons by baring his shoulders and whipping himself with chains, by clutching a crucifix and beating his chest with a rock, and by burning his flesh with candles. He did not

Spanish Landing Park

spare his native subjects. Once baptized, they were imprisoned and if disobedient, punished with the lash and stock.

The Spanish brought new diseases, and the Kumeyaay had no resistance. They died in droves. The friars and soldiers did not understand or respect the Kumeyaay methods of agriculture. Their cattle and horses destroyed the Kumeyaay fields. Perhaps the greatest humiliation, the soldiers made a sport of capturing and raping Kumeyaay women. The Kumeyaay could stand no more, and on November 5, 1775, by the light of a full moon, they attacked and burned the mission, killing a priest, Friar Luis Jayme, and two others.

Serra urged the soldiers to capture the attackers. He wrote Fernando de Rivera y Moncada, commander of the presidio in Spanish California's capital, Monterey.

San Diego Skyline from Coronado Ferry

First of all you should make them reflect on the great amount of evil they have done, then point out the severe punishment they deserve, and the undisputed power which our king and lord has to wipe them out of existence, as indeed they deserve. Point out that new soldiers have arrived and perhaps many more may be on their way, but that the aforesaid king, although mighty beyond compare, is also very Christian, that he has taken pity on them, etc.

I do not advocate that they be set free immediately, but that after they have been assured that their lives will be spared they should be freed according to the gravity of their crimes.

The soldiers rounded up those they deemed guilty, brought them to the San Diego presidio, and lashed them each 50 times. "Justice" for Indians was swift and ruthless in Colonial California.

Our trail continues along the shore of San Diego Bay and approaches downtown. The walkway comes alive with tourists, jewelry and t-shirt vendors, pedicabs, segways, exhibits, and historic ships. Catch the Coronado Ferry at Broadway Pier. (*http://coronadoferrylandingshops.com/san-diego-bay-ferry*) It leaves every hour and costs $4.25. A pedestrian ferry, its 15 minute journey is almost too short to take in the views of the San Diego waterfront and Coronado.

Restaurants and shops greet you as you disembark at the Coronado Ferry Landing. Stroll along the shoreline on the paved bike and walking path with stunning views of the city's skyline. Pass under the graceful arc of San Diego Coronado Bay Bridge.

Our trail passes through Tidelands Park, around Coronado Golf Club, by Coronado Yacht Basin, and into the village surrounding Hotel del Coronado. The hotel is worth a visit even if you don't stay there. It was built in 1888 and is one of largest and oldest

wooden structures in California. Stroll the grounds. Have a drink
at the outdoor bar on the edge of the wide Pacific beach. Then enjoy the many delights of the surrounding village – shops, bars with
live music, and restaurants with sidewalk tables.

Day 4: Coronado Village to Imperial Beach Pier

Hike through the grounds of Hotel del Coronado to the beach.
Look to the north and view your path over Point Loma and around
the mouth of San Diego Bay. Looking south, a curved beach
stretches twelve miles to the hills of Mexico. Now, set out for an
eight mile uninterrupted stroll along the Pacific.

If you start your hike around low tide or a few hours before,
you will be rewarded with a fine hiking surface, flat and firm, all
the way to Imperial Beach. Condominiums line the beach south of

Hotel del Coronado

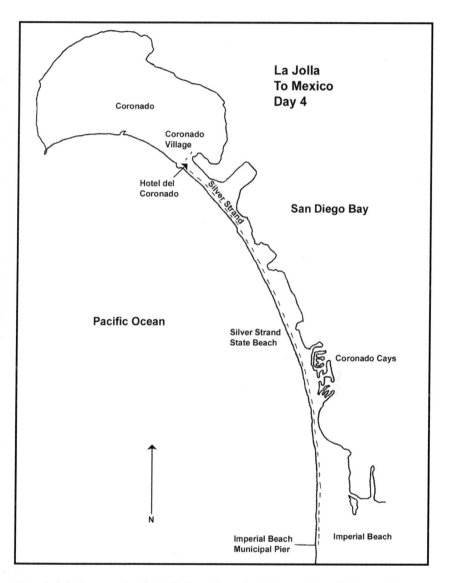

Coronado

Coronado Village

La Jolla
To Mexico
Day 4

Hotel del Coronado

Silver Strand

San Diego Bay

Pacific Ocean

Silver Strand
State Beach

Coronado Cays

N

Imperial Beach
Municipal Pier

Imperial Beach

Hotel del Coronado, but they end at the Navy's Amphibious Train-ing Base. The number of walkers and joggers dwindles, and soon you will probably have the beach to yourself.

You are hiking the Silver Strand, an eight-mile long and quarter-

Imperial Beach Surfer

mile wide strip of sand dune with a maximum elevation of around 25 feet. It connects Coronado and Imperial Beach, separating San Diego Bay from the Pacific. This is a good time to slow down and savor a long walk on a beautiful beach. There is no hurry.

The shore becomes busy again as you approach the campground and parking area of Silver Strand State Beach at 4.2 miles. A steady breeze blows off the Pacific making this a popular spot for kite surfers. Harnessed and tethered to large kites that look like a section of parachute, with feet strapped to a board, they ride the waves powered by the wind, cresting and soaring in the air, then screaming beyond the breakers at speeds of over 30 knots.

Leaving the state beach parking area, you once again have the shoreline to yourself. As we walked, we shared the next four miles with only flocks of snowy plover and marbled godwits feeding on kelp deposited on shore by the rising tide.

The beach was crowded around the pier on the early July afternoon we entered Imperial Beach. A slow moving, working class

A Moonrise Stroll on Hotel del Coronado Beach

town just a few miles from Mexico, it is a vivid contrast to the high-end villages of La Jolla and Coronado. The area around the pier has been recently renovated. We strolled through a lively farmers market featuring local produce and cuisine from around the world. People danced to the rhythm of a homegrown salsa band.

There are several restaurants along the waterfront. Take a long walk to the end of the pier and feast on fish tacos and crab cakes at Tin Fish Restaurant, or saddle up to the bar of IB Forum, "the most southwesterly bar and grill in the continental U.S.A.," for steaks, burgers, and seafood.

Day 5: Imperial Beach Pier to U.S./Mexico Border

The U.S./Mexico Border is only 3.3 miles south of Imperial Beach, a 6.6 mile round trip. Your path may be blocked by the Tijuana River at 1.7 miles, but it can be crossed in the dry season at low tide.

Condos line the beach for the first mile south of Imperial Beach Pier. As we walked, on a late July morning, the waves continued to be modest, only 2-3 feet. A few surfers and stand up paddle borders road the small breakers. Two fishermen cast lines into the surf. Other walkers strolled the shoreline to the river.

The estuary, marshland, and sand dunes of Border Field State Park flank the beach, a protected refuge for the endangered least tern and snowy plover. The river's mouth was crowded with pelicans, cormorants, gulls, egrets, terns, and plovers. The terns made an incredible racket, chattering and screeching.

Low tide is the best time to cross California rivers that flow to the sea. Sand bars form at their mouths, often making it possible to wade across.

The Tijuana River flows through Mexico and crowded Tijuana. Long plagued by pollution that sometimes flows into the Pacific after storms, the U.S. and Mexican governments have worked to-

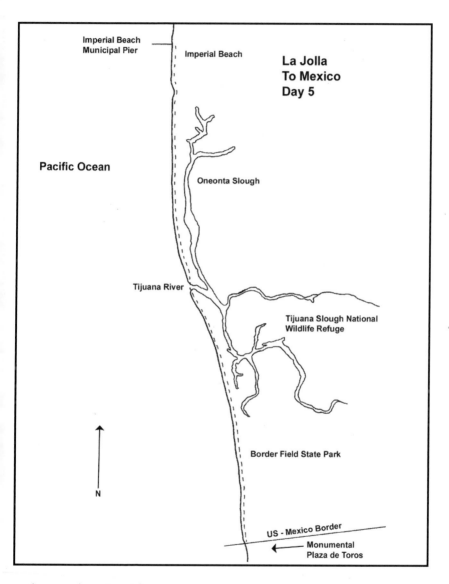

Imperial Beach Municipal Pier

Imperial Beach

La Jolla To Mexico Day 5

Pacific Ocean

Oneonta Slough

Tijuana River

Tijuana Slough National Wildlife Refuge

Border Field State Park

N

US - Mexico Border

Monumental Plaza de Toros

gether to clean it with some success.

Mexico and the border fence are clearly visible from the river, only 1.6 miles down the beach. Tall buildings and houses climb the hillside from the sea. The large stadium, Plaza de Toros Monumen-

Least Terns at Mouth of Tijuana River

tal de Tijuana, the Bullring by the Sea, stands high on a hill. The rocky Islas Coronados rises from the sea eight miles off the Mexican coast.

Hiking to the river would be a fitting end to this walkabout or to the 200 mile journey from Leo Carrillo State Beach along the magnificent Southern California Coast. We arrived an hour before low tide hoping to be able to cross going and returning. No rain had fallen for months, and the river ran clear and shallow. We took off our boots, tied them to our daypacks, and waded over the sandbar through waist deep water.

We shared the next 1.6 miles only with flocks of birds. An osprey glided up the shoreline, fifteen feet overhead.

The border fence is constructed of closely placed, 20 foot metal posts extending 100 yards into the sea. As we approached, we saw Mexican families on the other side enjoying a beautiful day at the beach. A man stood by the fence with a toddler in his arms. We greeted him and spoke briefly. His daughter reached through the fence and took Scott's hand, a sweet gesture of our natural desire to

Border Fence

reach across artificial boundaries.

This ends a five-day hike along the southwest shore of continental U.S.A. and a 200 mile adventure hiking inn-to-inn from north of Los Angeles to Mexico. It is a land of expansive beaches, rugged rocky coastlines, fun seaside towns, delightful inns, and surprisingly abundant wildlife. Take a walkabout – Malibu to Mexico – hiking inn-to-inn on the Southern California Coast.

THE ROUTE

The entire route of this five-day walkabout is passable at lower tides. If your passage is blocked by high tides, take one of the frequent paths or public stairs to briefly walk residential streets and return to the beach. Tide schedules are available at *http://tidesandcurrents.noaa.gov/tide_predictions.shtml.*

All mileages listed for a given day are cumulative.

Day 1: La Jolla to Crystal Pier, Pacific Beach

Leaving La Jolla Bay, hike the paved pathway along the coast and through Ellen Browning Scripps Park. Leave the paved pathway at Coast Blvd. Park and hike along the coastal rock shelves and beach to Windandsea Beach. Passage is blocked at the south end of Windandsea by a rocky promontory. Turn inland on the narrow public pathway at the end of the beach. ....**2.2 miles**

(If the tide is very high, the shoreline path may be blocked at Coast Blvd. Park. Walk on Coast Blvd., turn left on Pearl St., right on Olivetas, right on Marine St., left on Monte Vista Ave., right on Fern Glen, left on Neptune Place, left on Palomar, to Camino De La Costa.)

Turn right on Camino De La Costa, right on Chelsea Ave., right on Dolphin, right on Chelsea, left on Sea Ridge Dr. Take the stairway to the beach off of Sea Ridge Dr. across from Linda Way. ....**4.1 miles**

Pacific Beach Sand Castle

(The beach at the bottom of the stairs may be blocked at very high tide. In that case, continue on Sea Ridge Dr, turn right on Chelsea Ave., left on Wrelton Dr., right on La Jolla Blvd., and right on Tourmaline St. to the beach.) Hike the beach to Crystal Pier.. **total miles 5.1**

Day 2:
Crystal Pier, Pacific Beach to Shelter Island Yacht Basin

Walk south from Crystal Pier along the shore or the paved Ocean Front Walk to Belmont Park amusement park. It is easily spotted by street lights that now line Ocean Front Walk and by the wooden roller coaster. ....**1.7 miles**

Turn inland on Ventura Place to Mission Bay Park. Walk through the park angling between Bonita Cove on the right and Mariners Way on the left. Continue across the main channel of Mission Bay on West

Mexico

Mission Bay Drive bridge. Leaving the bridge, angle right through the park and walk around the Quivira Basin Yacht Harbor. Walk across the San Diego River on the Sunset Cliffs Blvd. bridge. Turn right immediately on the bike path along the river to the beach. ....**4.6 miles**

Turn left on the beach and hike to Ocean Beach Pier. ....**5.1 miles**

Walk the sidewalk under the base of Ocean Beach Pier to its end, descend a set of stairs, walk the coastal rock shelves for 0.3 miles, and ascend the first stairs to Santa Cruz Ave. Walk three blocks and turn right on Sunset Cliffs Blvd. (You may also choose to skip the coastal rock shelves and take Niagara Ave. directly from the pier and turn right on Sunset Cliffs Blvd.) Walk six blocks on Sunset Cliffs Blvd., turn left on Pt. Loma Ave. and cross over the crest of Pt. Loma Peninsula. Descend Pt. Loma Ave. to its end and turn left on Canon St. Turn left on Rosecrans St. and right on North Harbor Drive. The area around Rosecrans St. and North Harbor Dr. form the Shelter Island Yacht Basin neighborhood. This is where the inns listed in Places to Stay are located. .... **total miles 8.5**

Day 3: Shelter Island Yacht Basin to Coronado Village

Walk North Harbor Dr. around the north end of San Diego Bay. Continue along the bay through Spanish Landing Park. Walk the paved hiking and bike path rounding the east side of the bay to downtown San Diego and the Broadway Pier. .... **4.0 miles**

Take the Coronado Island Ferry. It leaves hourly and costs $4.25. Leaving the ferry, turn left and walk the paved pathway along the bay. Pass through the Coronado Tidelands Park and under the San Diego-Coronado Bridge. Turn right on the paved path at the Coronado Golf Course and left on Glorietta Blvd. bordering the golf course and past Coronado Yacht Club. You will see the towering Hotel del Coronado. Enter Coronado Village, the area surrounding the hotel. ....
.... **total miles 6.8**

Day 4: Coronado Village to Imperial Beach Municipal Pier

Walk through the grounds of Hotel del Coronado to the Pacific beach, turn left, and hike the shore to the Silver Strand State Beach parking area. ....**4.2 miles**

(The Navy's Amphibious Training Base is 0.6 miles south of Hotel del Coronado. You may not be allowed to hike this stretch of beach if the Navy is conducting training exercises. In that case, take the first street to Silver Strand Blvd., cross it, and hike the bike/walking path on the east side to Silver Strand State Beach.)

Continue along the Pacific shore to Imperial Beach Municipal Pier. .... **total miles 8.1**

Day 5: Imperial Municipal Beach Pier to U.S./Mexico Border

The Tijuana River may block your passage to the border. A sandbar forms at its mouth, and you can wade across at low tide during the dry season. Walk the beach south from Imperial Beach Pier to the Tijuana River. ....**1.7 miles**

Continue along the beach to the U.S./Mexico Border. .... **total miles 3.3**

TRANSPORTATION
Flying into San Diego

Take a Super Shuttle van from San Diego Airport to La Jolla. The cost is $29 for the first person and $9 for a second. For information and reservations call 800-258-3826 or try *www.supershuttle.com*. Super Shuttle also serves L.A. area airports.

Returning from Imperial Beach to La Jolla

Visit *www.transit.511sd.com* for easy public transportation trip planning. The combination bus and trolley ride that passes through Old Town San Diego should take about two hours and cost $2.25.

MAPS

The U.S. Geological Survey sells topographical hiking maps and provides free maps you can download. Visit *http://store.usgs.gov* and go to the map locator.

Day 1: La Jolla OE W Quadrangle

Day 2: La Jolla OE W Quadrangle, Point Loma Quadrangle

Day 3: Point Loma Quadrangle

Day 4: Point Loma Quadrangle, Imperial Beach OE W Quadrangle

Day 5: Imperial Beach OE W Quadrangle
Google Maps at *www.maps.google.com* is also a useful tool for viewing the shoreline and roadways adjacent to the shore.

PLACES TO STAY

LODGING COSTS

$ less than $100 | $$ $100-$150 | $$$ $150-$200 | $$$$ more than $200

La Jolla

These are a few of the many places to stay

Inn by the Sea Best Western Plus
7830 Fay Ave.
858-459-4461
www.bestwestern.com
$$-$$$$

Empress Hotel
7766 Fay Ave.
858-454-3001
www.empress-hotel.com
$$-$$$$

La Valencia Hotel
1132 Prospect St.
858-454-0771
www.lavalencia.com
$$$$

La Jolla Cove Suites
1155 Coast Blvd.
858-459-2621
www.lajollacove.com
$$-$$$$

Hotel del Coronado Dining

Pacific Beach

Ocean Park Inn
710 Grand Ave.
800-483-5858
www.oceanparkinn.com
$-$$$$

Crystal Pier Hotel and Cottages
4500 Ocean Blvd.
858-483-6983
www.crystalpier.com
$$$-$$$$

Banana Bungalow Hostel
707 Reed Ave.
858-273-3060
www.bananabungalowsandiego.com
$

Beach Cottages
4255 Ocean Blvd.
848-483-7440
www.beachcottages.com
$$$-$$$$

Catamaran Resort and Spa
3999 Mission Blvd.
858-488-4081
www.catamaranresort.com
$$$-$$$$

Mission Bay Motel
4221 Mission Blvd.
858-483-6440
www.missionbaymotel.com
$-$$$

Blue Sea Lodge
707 Pacific Beach Dr.
800-488-4700
www.bestwestern-bluesea.com
$$-$$$$

Shelter Island Yacht Basin

Holiday Inn San Diego Bayside
4875 No. Harbor Dr.
619-224-3621
www.holidayinn.com
$$-$$$$

Vagabond Inn
1325 Scott St.
619-224-3371
www.vagabondinn.com
$-$$$

Best Western Yacht Harbor Hotel
5005 N. Harbor Dr.
619-224-3254
www.yachtharborhotel.com
$$-$$$

Sheraton San Diego Hotel and Marina
1380 Harbor Island Dr.
619-291-2900
www.sheratonsandiegohotel.com
$$$-$$$$

Comfort Inn at the Harbor
5102 No. Harbor Dr.
619-223-8171
www.comfortinnattheharbor.com
$-$$$

Coronado Village

Hotel del Coronado
1500 Orange Ave.
800-468-3533
www.hoteldel.com
$$$$

La Avenida Inn
1315 Orange Ave.
800-437-0162
www.laavenidainn.com
$$-$$$$

Glorietta Bay Inn
1630 Glorietta Blvd.
619-435-3101
www.gloriettabayinn.com
$$-$$$$

El Cordova Hotel
1351 Orange Ave.
619-435-4131
www.elcordovahotel.com
$$-$$$$

1906 Lodge at Coronado Beach
1060 Adella Ave.
619-437-1900
www.1906lodge.com
$$$$

Coronado Island Marriot Resort and Spa
2000 Second St.
619-435-3000
www.marriott.com
$$$$
Between the ferry landing and Coronado Village

Imperial Beach

Sand Castle Inn
785 Seacoast Dr.
619-429-4796
www.sandcastlevacation.com
$$$

Pier South
800 Seacoast Dr.
619-621-5900
www.piersouthresort.com
$$$$

Notes

Index

Index

Index

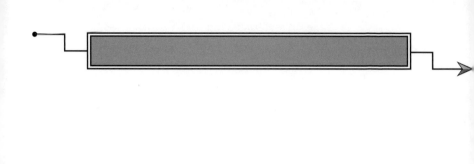

TOM COURTNEY is the author of "Walkabout Northern California – Hiking Inn to Inn," a book of self-guided inn-to-inn hikes through the wilds of Northern California. With only a light daypack, you can hike on California's breathtaking coastline or in the Sierra Nevada Mountains ending each day with a hot shower, a delicious meal, a comfortable bed, and maybe even a hot tub. Tom recently retired from teaching at the University of California, Berkeley and consulting with nonprofit organizations. He now devotes his time to writing, hiking, and speaking. Tom and his wife, Heidi, live in Oakland, CA.

STAY IN TOUCH
The Walkabout California community is growing, and there are so many more inn-to-inn hikes to be discovered in California. We continue to explore, and so do others. Join the discussion about inn-to-inn hiking at *WalkaboutCalifornia.com*. Share your questions, reviews of restaurants and inns that you enjoyed along the journey, photos, and favorite moments from the trail. Find out about new walkabouts, and share in the adventure.